By Tina Houser

Unless otherwise noted, Scripture quotations are from the ESV® Bible (The Holy Bible, English Standard Version®), copyright © 2001 by Crossway Bibles, a publishing ministry of Good News Publishers. Used by permission. All rights reserved.

©2014 by Warner Press Inc Anderson, IN 46018

www.warnerpress.org

All rights reserved

ISBN: 978-1-59317-770-6

No part of this publication may be reproduced, stored in a retrieval system, or transmitted in any form or by any means—electronic, mechanical, photocopy, recording, or any other—except for brief quotations in printed reviews, without the prior permission of the publisher.

Editor: Karen Rhodes

Photography: Kevin DeHoff

Design & Illustrations: Christian Elden

Printed in USA

829850110093

Table of Contents

Meet Dr. Bunsenburner 2

Who is this book for? 3

Thanks for Making This Happen! 6

Balance Board 8
    Balance in your life

Balloon in a Bottle 11
    Weakness

Through a Balloon 14
    Trials

Bubble Stream 16
    God Is Able

Bubbles, Bubbles, and More Bubbles 19
    Gentleness / Being Prepared

Can't Crush This 22
    Hope

Can't Let Go 25
    Love of money

Coin Drop 27
    Rest

Cola or Diet Cola 29
    Obeying God's Word

Cola-rized Egg 31
    Forgiveness

Color Transfer 33
    Serving

Disappearing Eggshell 36
    Life change

Draw All Men 38
    Drawn to Jesus

Dropping Hex Nuts 41
    Rescue

Egg in a Bottle 43
    Drawn Near to God

Egg Prints 46
    Love

Eggs-traordinary Strength 49
    God's Promises

Elephant Toothpaste 52
    Praise

Energy Stick 55
    Sharing the Gospel

Floating Ms 58
    God Doesn't See Labels

Floating Paper Clip 60
    Advice

Fuzzy Magnet 63
    Individual Gifts

Boiling Mad 66
    Anger

He's Not Here! 69
    Jesus' resurrection

High Bouncer 71
    God's ways

Hovering Bottle 73
    Jesus' Birth

Hovering Ping-Pong Ball 75
    Witnessing

On and On 78
    Don't continue to sin

Hidden Potential 80
    The future

Kool-Aid Bursts™ Launch 82
    Evangelism

Lava Lamp 85
    Alive in Christ

Lift Up a Plate 88
    Humble yourself

Lifting Up Praise 91
    Preparing to worship

Light and Relight 94
    Resurrection

Light Bulb in Microwave 97
    Living in the Light

Forget Their Sins 99
    God forgets our sins

One Breath 102
    Confession

Ping-Pong® Wiggle 105
    Unity

Pull Harder 108
    Nothing can separate us

Make a Joyful Noise 110
    Praise

Rising Match 113
    Heaven

Separating the Egg 116
    Separate from Sin

Shrinky Dinky Cup 118
    Under pressure

Spilled Out 121
    Love spills out

Spinning Chair 124
    Hold God close

Stacking Surprise 126
    Trust God

Standing Broom 129
    Stand up for your faith

Stomp Rocket 131
    Witnessing

Suspended Support 135
    Bear one another's burdens

Swinging Bucket 138
    Trust God's Word

Temptation Sand 141
    Temptation

Unbreakable 144
    Relying on God's strength

Upside Down 146
    Jesus brings change

Water Stream 149
    Unity

Scripture Index 152

Meet Dr. Bunsenburner

Welcome to my laboratory! I am Dr. Fran Bunsenburner, and in my special laboratory we observe science experiments in order to learn more about the Word of God. Thanks for joining me for this new volume of amazing science experiments and discussions.

Please don't ask me to explain the science behind each experiment. I really don't know why things bubble over...or shoot off into the sky...or shrink...or hang upside down mysteriously...or make you scratch your head and scrunch your eyebrows. I do love to watch it happen, though. The challenge, then, is observing the experiment, and discovering how we can relate it to God's precious book.

I love the Word of God and I love helping kids grasp its meaning. Sometimes that means getting a little creative and going to extremes—like donning an outlandish hairstyle and talking with a crazy accent. At the core of it is my deep desire to turn the hearts of kids toward the God Who created them, Who will take them on an amazing journey that begins now, but lasts through eternity.

In His incredible joy,

Dr. Fran Bunsenburner

(aka Tina Houser)

Who is this book for?

Children's Ministry Workers

Science is fascinating, so kids naturally gravitate to it. If you're teaching 3rd-6th grade boys and they're just about to push you over the edge (which they're really good at), then bring out a science experiment. Their attention will immediately focus on what you're doing and will lead them into a great discussion. Why? Because you have tapped into their fascination factor.

Although we tend to think that abstract thinking—in this case, connecting a physical experience to a biblical concept—is something for older kids, it's actually a skill that can be learned early on if we give kids experience in this thinking process. Science experiments are object lessons, pure and simple, when used in this manner. And, most people wholeheartedly agree that object lessons are valuable.

I had a preschool teacher share with me that some of her 4-year-old students are so visual, and so high in their picture intelligence, that if a lesson doesn't have an object lesson or science experiment in it, those students have a difficult time retaining the meaning behind the Bible story. The science experiment is the one thing they can explain when parents ask, "What did you learn today?"

Science experiments add the pizzazz to a mundane lesson and get kids excited! Seek out opportunities during Sunday school, kids' church, midweek program, or special event to make something bubble over, blow up, or just amaze your kids with jaw-dropping surprises using science.

Homeschoolers

This volume of science experiments provides a unique opportunity for homeschoolers. Each one of these experiments gives you all the instructions you need to set up the experiment and observe it. It also provides you with a connection to Scripture so you can have a great discussion with your kids about God's Word. But then, it's in your court. We've presented you with an open door to teach the science ... the why's, what if's, and how's that go right along with each scientific principle being demonstrated. Rather than Bible study time, family time, teaching time, and science class being separate activities, these experiments incorporate all of them, in one lesson.

Parents

Family devotions can be a challenging holy habit to get into. That's usually because everyone looks at it as a boring activity. Each one of these experiments will be fun FOR EVERY MEMBER of the family and give you something to do TOGETHER. Families don't spend time involved in common experiences, but you can now, and even make it something that everyone looks forward to with anticipation.

Getting your kids excited about science and the Word of God is great. Keep encouraging them to stretch their science knowledge and let that knowledge drive them deeper into the Scriptures.

Last year I spoke with a woman who bought *Beakers, Bubbles and the Bible, Volume 1* a year before. She took it home so she and her husband could do the experiments with their middle elementary son. He could not get enough! In fact, it sparked a real love for science, so much so that they redesigned their sunroom (adding heating and cooling) to be a designated science room for him. She reported that he was now teaching his little sister, using all the science experiments.

Grandparents

So many Christian grandparents are troubled that their grandchildren are not attending church or being raised in a home where the One True God is honored and worshiped. When those grandchildren are in their care, they want to somehow pour their faith story into them. How cool would you be as a grandparent if the next time your grandkids came over you made some "Elephant Toothpaste," creating a tower of dense foam! Take advantage of the moment you have created. Open your Bibles together around the "Discussion" included with each experiment and tell them how your walk with God reflects the topic.

Another great resource for grandparents is *More Than Cookies and Punch*, where you make snacks together that go along with a Bible story.

Pastors

One thing that always puzzles me is why pastors think they need to be so stiff and limit themselves to one way of communicating. They confine themselves to words and 3 major points in their sermons. What happens if someone visits your church for the very first time and they're not word smart? People think in

pictures and that's exactly where science experiments fall. If your topic for the morning is how Christians should be turning the world upside down in a radical way, then demonstrate the "Upside Down" experiment. Your people will remember what you were talking about and will be super anxious to get home and try it themselves. What an opportunity to talk about the sermon with their kids or co-workers as they amaze them with this experiment.

This book is for...
ANYONE WHO NEEDS AN ATTENTION GRABBER!

If you lead a Life Group, Bible study, speak for a club, or need to somehow get a group's attention, a science experiment does the trick. It not only pulls people together, but it gives them something memorable to take with them.

Thanks for Making This Happen!

Well, **Lord**, you opened yet another door. My prayer remains that You give me the good sense if there's an opportunity knocking at my door that I at least have the good sense to open it to see who's there. Thanks for allowing me to serve You as I serve Your kids. **Warner Press** knocked on the door again, and I thank You for all the crazy things You passed through my brain as I prepared this work.

If you know me, you'll quickly realize as you go through the book that the hands holding the experiments are not mine. Even though both of my hands have been totally reconstructed, 40 years with crippling rheumatoid arthritis is still quite evident. My lovely daughter-in-law, **Kelley**, graciously became the hand model for the book, as well as demonstrated a few of the experiments. Thanks so much, Kelley. I owe you a manicure!

The adorable kids throughout the book are **Bowen and Kendall**, my grandtwins, who are five. They are my "Happy Place" whenever I need to step away from responsibilities. As you can probably imagine, science experiments are a regular part of time spent at Silly Grandma's house—a name they chose. Thanks for spending a day in front of a camera so I could show you off (which is my duty as President of the Obnoxious Grandparents' Club).

The book would not have communicated the experiments well if it hadn't been for **Kevin DeHoff**, photographer and youth pastor at Shorewood Church of God. It was a long day of snapping shots of experiment after experiment, with lots… and I do mean lots…of laughter throughout. Thanks for making this an easy-to-understand resource!

Before we get on with checking out experiments, none of this could happen without the incredible support I get from the two men in my life—my husband **Ray** and son **Jarad**. In their own ways, they both challenge me to do more and go further than I think possible. They both honor me far more than I deserve; it's beyond a privilege to call them husband and son.

ALWAYS TEST THE EXPERIMENT BEFORE YOU PRESENT IT.

Balance Board
Balance in your life

Scripture:

Ecclesiastes 3:1-8 (ESV)

*For everything there is a season, and a time for every matter under heaven:
a time to be born, and a time to die;
a time to plant, and a time to pluck up what is planted;
a time to kill, and a time to heal;
a time to break down, and a time to build up;
a time to weep, and a time to laugh;
a time to mourn, and a time to dance;
a time to cast away stones, and a time to gather stones together;
a time to embrace, and a time to refrain from embracing;
a time to seek, and a time to lose;
a time to keep, and a time to cast away;
a time to tear, and a time to sew;
a time to keep silence, and a time to speak;
a time to love, and a time to hate;
a time for war, and a time for peace.*

Lab Equipment

- 2-liter bottle
- old skateboard
- screwdriver
- water

Experiment

- Remove the wheels and any housing from an old skateboard. You only want the board for this exercise.

- Fill an empty 2-liter bottle with water. The best way to do this is to hold it under water in a tub. This will actually keep even tiny air bubbles from being in the bottle. Screw the cap on while the bottle is still underwater to ensure it is completely full.

- Just for safety's sake, let someone else tighten the cap, also, if he or she can.

- Lay the bottle on the floor on its side. Set the board across it.
- Step onto the board and experiment with how you can make the board move under your feet while you balance yourself.

Observation

- How difficult was it to stand on the board?
- What happened when you put too much weight on one end of the board?
- Did it get easier with practice?
- What do you think you would be able to do on this board if you practiced 15 minutes every day?
- What happened when you tried to push too far and do something crazy?

Discussion

- Read Ecclesiastes 3:1-8.
- How does the balance board remind you of these verses?
- What does it mean to keep your life in balance?
  (It means that you don't overdo in one area and neglect something else that's important.)
- As long as you stayed balanced, you didn't fall off the balance board. What happened when you put too much weight on one end?
- When have you felt that your life was out of balance? How does it feel when that happens? Are you spending too much time playing video games and not taking care of chores, or homework, or practicing what your coach said? Are you so into sports that you neglect going to church?
- How does our life balance change?
  (When unexpected things happen, we may have to change what we're giving a lot of time to, at least for a while.)

- Choose one line from the Scripture passage (like, "a time to mourn, and a time to dance"). Tell when you have experienced both of those.

Other verses to use with this experiment:
- Luke 2:52
- Ephesians 5:15

Balloon in a Bottle
Weakness

Scripture:

John 13:37-38 (ESV)

Peter said to him, "Lord, why can I not follow you now? I will lay down my life for you." Jesus answered, "Will you lay down your life for me? Truly, truly, I say to you, the rooster will not crow till you have denied me three times."

Lab Equipment

- balloon
- empty water bottle

Experiment

- Ask a big, strong volunteer to try to blow up a balloon. Then, double-check his commitment to being able to do this.

- Hand the volunteer a balloon, and right as he begins to blow it up, stop him and say there was one detail you forgot to mention.

- Place the balloon down in an empty water bottle and pull the lip of the balloon over the mouth of the bottle. The balloon should be hanging down inside the bottle, with the top securely wrapped around the mouth of the bottle.

- Now, ask the volunteer to blow up the balloon. He will not be able to do this. Urge him on, reminding him that he said he could blow up a balloon when you asked him.

- Before the volunteer passes out from over-exerting himself trying to blow up the balloon, inform him that he won't be able to do it.

Observation

- How did our volunteer feel about blowing up the balloon when we first began?

- What change affected the way the balloon could be blown up?
- What happened when the volunteer blew into the balloon?
- How did the volunteer react when he couldn't do what he said?

Discussion

- Read John 13:37-38. You may need to read some of the verses prior to this to get the entire picture of what is happening.

- When the disciples are having the meal with Jesus, what does Peter proclaim he will do? Does he seem sure about the fact that he has declared he will never deny knowing Jesus?

- What are the circumstances at the dinner? Who is there? Does Peter feel safe with the disciples and Jesus?

- Out in the crowd, one thing had changed that affected how Peter reacted when asked if he knew Jesus. What one thing changed? The soldiers had taken Jesus.
  It wasn't such a safe environment now!

- Why do you think Peter said three different times that he didn't know Jesus—that he wasn't one of Jesus' followers?

- Have you ever had a time when you were sure you wouldn't lie, or you wouldn't take something that didn't belong to you, or you would stand up for someone who was in trouble…and then when the time came, you weren't able to do what you thought you could do? Tell about one of those times. How did you feel about what you did? How do you think Peter felt when the rooster crowed and he realized what he had done?

- Our volunteer was absolutely sure he could blow up a balloon, but when one circumstance changed—we put

the balloon inside the bottle—he wasn't able to do it. Sometimes, we're sure we know how strong we will be, then one circumstance changes and we're a lot weaker than we thought. God understands our weaknesses. Jesus realized Peter's weakness even before he told the first person he didn't know Jesus. Jesus knew how it broke Peter's heart to disappoint Him like that, and Jesus was also there to give Peter a second chance.

- Peter messed up! He didn't stand up for Jesus. He failed. But, do you know who Peter became? He became a leader of the Church. He was one of the main people God used to spread the word all over the world that Jesus is God's Son, the Savior for the world.

Other verse to use with this experiment:
- 2 Corinthians 12:9-11

Through a Balloon
Trials

Scripture:

Joshua 1:9 (ESV)

Have I not commanded you? Be strong and courageous. Do not be frightened, and do not be dismayed, for the Lord your God is with you wherever you go.

Lab Equipment

- fine sand paper
- large balloon
- soft cloth
- thin wooden skewer
- vegetable oil

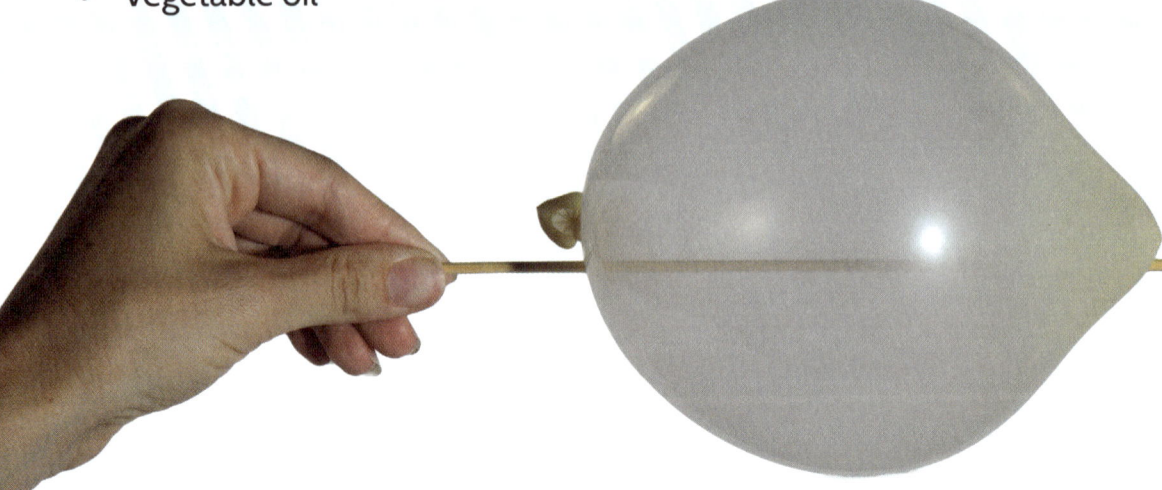

Experiment

- Prepare a thin wooden skewer by lightly sanding it with fine sandpaper. Wipe it off with a soft cloth.

- Dip the skewer in vegetable oil and wipe again.

- Blow a large balloon up to about 75% full.

- Push the skewer through the balloon at a place close to the knot, where the latex is thick.

- Go through the balloon with the skewer and then push it out the other side (at the bottom of the balloon), where the latex is concentrated.

Observation

- What words would you use to describe a balloon normally?
- What did you expect to happen?
- How would you describe this balloon?
- Was this a special balloon? (No)

Discussion

- Read Joshua 1:9.
- How does this scripture remind you of the experiment we just did with the balloon?
- Do you ever feel fragile, like you could fall apart, or like with one poke you could pop?
- How does it make you feel to know God is with you wherever you go? He never leaves you. He's always there!
- Name something you've gotten tired of. Without naming the person, have you had a friend in the past that you got tired of hanging out with? Does God get tired of you? Never! God doesn't hit and run. He doesn't show up, pat you on the back, give you a pep talk, and then head on His way. No! He shows up to go with you through whatever it is you're facing. He will not turn His back on you. He won't get tired of you! He won't leave you.
- You thought the balloon was going to pop when it got poked with the skewer, but it didn't. God also will amaze you as He takes you through some pretty crazy situations.

Other verses to use with this experiment:
- John 16:33
- Acts 14:22
- James 1:2

Bubble Stream
God Is Able

Scripture:

Ephesians 3:20 (ESV)

Now to him who is able to do far more abundantly than all that we ask or think, according to the power at work within us.

Lab Equipment

- box cutter
- cheap bubble solution
- old, thin washcloth
- rubber band
- scissors
- shallow pan
- water
- water bottle

Experiment

- Use a box cutter to cut a plastic water bottle in half. For this experiment you will be using the top half with the mouth of the bottle. (The bottom half can be used for all kinds of things, so don't toss it–plant starter, cup for paints, sand scoop/mold.)

- Cut a piece of an old, thin terry washcloth about 5" x 5".

- Dampen the cloth and wring it out really well. Squeeze, squeeze, squeeze!

- Lay the piece of washcloth over the big open end of the water bottle and secure it in place with a strong rubber band.

- Pour some bubble solution into a shallow pan. Any cheap bubble solution will work.

- Dip the terry-covered end of the water bottle in the solution. Pick it up and hold it over the pan until the bubble solution is no longer dripping.

- Now comes the really fun part! Blow into the mouth of the bottle.

A steady mass of tiny little bubbles will flow out of the washcloth! (For preschoolers, practice blowing OUT before blowing into the bottle, or they will inevitably suck in and get a mouthful of bubble solution. A good way to prepare them is to light a candle, have them suck in air, h-o-l-d it for 3 seconds and then blow out the candle. Another way to practice blowing is to have them put their finger about an inch from their mouth to feel the difference between sucking in air and blowing out air.) Making a bubble solution with extra dishwashing liquid in it will create a denser, whiter bubble stream.

Observation

- What do you usually use to make bubbles?
- How did these bubbles look different?
- How many bubbles did this special bubble maker make?
- What was needed in order for the bubbles to be made?

Discussion

- Read Ephesians 3:20.
- What one word *hits* you in this verse? What word sticks out or is your favorite? There are no right or wrong answers...just curious.
- What connection do you make between the experiment and this verse?
- Have you ever gone somewhere to see something you'd never seen before and when you actually saw it, it was bigger and better than

you had imagined? When was that? Maybe you visited the Grand Canyon and before you left, you looked at pictures and your parents told you it was really big. But, then, when you got there and looked over the railing, you said, "WOW! This is the biggest thing I've ever seen! It's gargantuan!" It's so much bigger than you had even imagined it could be.

- When we pray and ask God to take care of situations, we only think about how we can imagine it being taken care of. Blowing bubbles is usually done one at a time, but this flow of bubbles, was more than we were expecting. There were a lot more bubbles—a cool stream of them—than we thought were going to come out. God has endless possibilities and can handle our situations in ways we cannot imagine. What if we prayed, "God, here's my situation. Take it and do something big that only You can do! I'm ready to be amazed," *instead* of telling God how we'd like for Him to work.

- This scripture reminds us that God is able to do FAR MORE ABUNDANTLY than we can even imagine. When has God done something that totally blew your mind?

Other verses to use with this experiment:
- John 10:10
- 2 Corinthians 9:8

Bubbles, Bubbles, and More Bubbles

Gentleness / Being Prepared

Scripture:

1 Peter 3:15 (ESV)

But in your hearts honor Christ the Lord as holy, always being prepared to make a defense to anyone who asks you for a reason for the hope that is in you; yet do it with gentleness and respect.

Lab Equipment

- bubble solution
- cotton candy tubes (or see how to make your own below)
- drinking straw
- empty water bottle
- plastic container

If you want to make your own paper cone, you will need thick construction paper, clear tape, scissors, pencil, string, and a ruler. Tie a string to a pencil so the length from the end of the string to the pencil is about 8". Hold the free end of the string in the corner of a piece of construction paper. Pull the pencil away from the corner until the string is taut. Set the pencil point down on the paper and pull the pencil around to mark a quarter-circle on the paper. Cut this out. Roll it into a cone shape, aligning the bottom edge and leaving just a small hole at the top of the cone. Tape it securely, inside and outside.

Experiment

- Point out and verbalize the steps you take to make this experiment happen. Choose one of the bubble solutions on page 15. These are all stronger than the cheap bubbles you get at a department store. Pour a small amount of the solution in a plastic container—no more than ¼" deep. You need a container that is big enough to set the end of your paper cone in.

- Fill a water bottle with the bubble solution.

- If your cotton candy paper cone does not have a small hole at the tip, then snip the tip off. This will give you a place to blow into your bubble maker.

- Set the base of the cotton candy cone in the plastic container for a few seconds to let the paper slightly absorb some of the bubble solution.

- Lift the cone out and gently blow into the small opening at the tip. You should get a good-sized bubble that doesn't break easily. This is fun...but there's more!

- Push a straw through one of the bubbles. It will break.

- Drop the straw down into the water bottle full of bubble solution.

- The next step is easiest if you have a helper. The other person will pull the straw out of the water bottle. When a bubble is blown, the helper will push the straw through the bubble–in one side and out the other. The distance the straw will go through the bubble depends on how long you let the straw soak in the bubble solution.

- Now, have loads of fun!

Observation

- What did we have to do to get ready to make these bubbles?

- What happened the first time we tried to put the straw through the bubble?

- What did we have to do to prepare the straw to go through the bubble?

- How did the helper treat the bubble when he put the straw through it? (gently)

- What surprised you about these bubbles?

Discussion

- In our experiment, what did we have to prepare? (We prepared a good bubble solution.) What happened to the bubble when we didn't prepare the straw to go through it? What was the difference once the straw had been prepared properly?

- Read 1 Peter 3:15.
- According to this verse, what do we need to be prepared for? We need to be prepared for questions people may ask us about our faith. We need to be prepared to tell someone about how Jesus has changed our lives. We need to be prepared to stand up for our beliefs. How else should we be prepared?
- Does this mean that we get in arguments or get mad if someone doesn't agree with us? Does it mean that we make him feel stupid if he doesn't believe also?
- How are we supposed to talk to other people about Jesus? What kind of attitude should we have? (The last few words of this verse tell us. We should tell others about Jesus with "gentleness and respect.")
- So, after talking about all that, let's think about our bubbles again and how we got the straw to go through them. How was our experiment like what 1 Peter 3:15 says about how we should talk with others? We pushed the straw through the bubble gently. It would be wise if we kept that same gentleness in mind when we tell others about our wonderful Jesus!

Bubble Solution #1

- ¼ cup Steve Spangler Extreme Bubble Solution
- 2 cups distilled water
- 1 T white Karo syrup

Bubble Solution #2

- ½ cup dishwashing liquid (Dawn or Joy)
- 4 T glycerin (available at a hobby store)
- 5 cups distilled water
- 1 T Karo syrup

Super Bubble Solution

- 3 parts dish soap (Dawn or Joy)
- 5 parts glycerin
- 1 part Karo syrup
- (no water)

Other verse to use with this experiment:
- James 1:2-4

Can't Crush This
Hope

Scripture:

2 Corinthians 4:7-9 (ESV)

But we have this treasure in jars of clay, to show that the surpassing power belongs to God and not to us. We are afflicted in every way, but not crushed; perplexed, but not driven to despair; persecuted, but not forsaken; struck down, but not destroyed.

Lab Equipment

- raw egg

Experiment

- Remove any rings from your fingers before doing this.

- Place a raw egg in the palm of your hand and wrap your fingers around it. Keep the pads of your fingers flat against the egg. You do not want to have your fingertips curled going into the egg.

- Squeeze as hard as you can. (If you are not confident in what will happen, then put a drop cloth under your hand or do this over a sink.) The egg will not break.

Observation

- Do you always check eggs at the grocery store before buying them? Why is that?

- How did the person who was going to squeeze the egg appear when she was told what she was going to do?

- What did you expect to happen?
- What happened when the person squeezed the egg?
- Were you convinced they were really squeezing?

Discussion

- Read 2 Corinthians 4:7-9. How does this verse remind you of our experiment with the raw egg?
- What are the opposites in these verses?
- When we're afflicted that usually means we're really down (crushed by our situation), but verse 8 says that God's power keeps that from happening to us. God's power keeps us from being crushed by our situation!
- When someone has questions and they're confused, they may get depressed or give up. God's power, though, can keep us from depression and despair.
- When someone is being persecuted, you'd think they would feel abandoned and lonely, like no one is there to help (forsaken). But, what does verse 9 say? God's power keeps us from feeling forsaken.
- When everything seems to be going wrong and you're not getting any breaks, when you feel "struck down," on your own power, the circumstances make you feel like giving up. But God's power keeps you from being destroyed by what's happening to you, no matter how rotten you think things are going.
- We normally think of an egg as being fragile–that it breaks easily. Many times, we can feel like a fragile egg. But verse 7 reminds us that we don't have to rely on our own power to get through life. It says that the power is not OURS. The surpassing power belongs to God! Surpassing means that it's beyond any other power–waaaaay beyond! When you feel fragile, no matter how many crazy things are pressing in on you, you can know that God has surpassing power over it. If you claim His power, then you won't be "crushed...driven to despair...forsaken...destroyed." Woo-Hoo! and Amen!

Try This Extra!
- Put a ring on the hand you're squeezing with and see what happens to the egg.
- Curl your fingertips into the egg as you squeeze, instead of keeping them flat.
- Just a forewarning, you will want to do these with a drop cloth or over the sink and have a rag handy!

Other verses to use with this experiment:
- Psalm 18:32
- Psalm 28:7
- Joshua 1:9
- Philippians 4:13

Can't Let Go
Love of money

Scripture:

Matthew 19:21-22 (ESV)

Jesus said to him, "If you would be perfect, go, sell what you possess and give to the poor, and you will have treasure in heaven; and come, follow me." When the young man heard this he went away sorrowful, for he had great possessions.

Lab Equipment

- a quarter

Experiment

- Put your hands, fingers extended and palms together, completely flat against one another.
- Bend your middle fingers forward across the back of the opposing hand.
- Get a partner to slide a quarter between your ring fingers.
- Try to let go of the quarter by pulling the ring fingers away from each other.

Observation

- How difficult was it for the person to get their hands pressed together in the position?
- What happened when the person tried to pull the ring fingers apart?
- How difficult was it to let go of the quarter? Was the person able to do it?

Discussion

- Read Matthew 19:16-24, the story of the young man who approached Jesus with a question about what he needed to do to receive eternal life.
- Which of God's laws had the man followed?

- Jesus recognized that the man still had a problem. What was it? (He wasn't willing to let go of his money. His money was even more important than having eternal life.)

- The point Jesus was making with the man was that God must always have the highest position in our lives. Nothing should ever be more important than obeying God. Was God the most important part of this man's life? What was most important to the man?

- How did our experiment remind you of this story from the Bible?

- You think it wouldn't be that difficult to let go of the quarter, but when it comes down to really doing it, it is super difficult. How is that like our attitude toward the money we have? What do we think we will do with it? What do we actually end up doing with it?

- Does this mean that having money is bad? How can money be a good thing?

- How can we use our money to honor God and show Him that He is most important in our lives?

- When has it been difficult for you to let go of money? In order to honor God, we have to be willing to let go of our money when it can help others know about Jesus.

Other verses to use with this experiment:
- Job 30:13 (The Message)
- Matthew 6:19-21
- 1 Timothy 6:10
- Hebrews 13:5

Coin Drop
Rest

Scripture:

Matthew 11:28-29

Come to me, all who labor and are heavy laden, and I will give you rest. Take my yoke upon you, and learn from me, for I am gentle and lowly in heart, and you will find rest for your souls.

Lab Equipment

- juice glass
- nickel
- poster board
- water

Experiment

- Cut a piece of poster board into a 4" square.
- Fill a juice glass about two-thirds full of water.
- Lay the poster board square over the juice glass.
- Set the nickel in the middle of the square.
- You are going to knock the square out from under the nickel by flicking it with your finger. You need to make sure you're going straight on and that it's a firm and powerful flick. Practice a couple of times with an empty glass and no nickel. The square should not fly into the air, but go forward in the same plane as how it's laying on the glass.

Observation

- What happened to the nickel when you got the square out of the way?
- Describe how the nickel landed.
- How many times did you have to practice before you were able to knock the square out of the way?

- Did it get easier once you got the hang of it?

Discussion

- Read Matthew 11:28-29.

- How do the experiment and this scripture relate to one another?

- In the experiment, what represents us? (The nickel. We're stuck because something is in our way.)

- What does the square represent? (It's the things that get in our way–our obstacles.)

- How do we get those things–those obstacles and the stress that goes with them–out of the way? Jesus says to give them to Him. When we do, Jesus knocks them out of the way! And, what will He give us when we hand over our heavy stuff? He gives us rest.

- Did the nickel fall hard or was it a gentle landing? When the nickel hit the water, it didn't thud to the bottom; it gently floated down to the bottom, like it was cushioned. How does Jesus describe Himself in verse 29?

- When have you needed rest? I'm not talking about a nap, but when have things maybe been stressful or overwhelming and you needed to feel some peace inside?

- It takes practice to hand over our stress. Just like it took some practice to be able to knock the square out of the way, we have to get in the habit of handing things over to Jesus. We want to just leave things the way they are, but that's not going to get us anywhere. That nickel would've laid there forever if we hadn't knocked the square out of the way! Once we experience the rest that Jesus gives when we hand our obstacles over to Him, it's easier to do it the next time.

Other verses to use with this experiment:
- Matthew 6:13
- 1 Corinthians 10:13
- Philippians 4:6-7

Cola or Diet Cola
Obeying God's Word

Scripture:

1 John 5:3-4 (ESV)

For this is the love of God, that we keep his commandments. And his commandments are not burdensome. For everyone who has been born of God overcomes the world. And this is the victory that has overcome the world—our faith.

Lab Equipment

- aquarium or large tub
- can of cola
- can of diet cola
- water

Experiment

- Fill an aquarium at least two-thirds full. You want a nice full tank of water. The aquarium works best for this because the kids can see through the sides, but if you don't have an aquarium available, use a large tub. The children will have to stand around it, though.

- Place the can of cola in the aquarium at the surface and let go. Make sure any water bubbles under the can are released.

- Place the can of diet cola in the aquarium at the surface of the water and let go. Make sure any water bubbles under the can are released.

Observation

- What happened to the can of cola?

- What happened to the can of diet cola?

- Which of these surprised you?

Discussion

- Let's say the cola can is the person who makes poor decisions and does not obey God's Word. This person doesn't feel it's important to obey God's Word, and because of that, he makes poor decisions. How does the cola can in the aquarium remind you of the person who disobeys God's Word? I don't know about you, but I don't like sinking! When we disobey God's Word, our lives have that sinking feeling.

- And the diet cola can represents the person who obeys God's Word and makes wise decisions. He values what the Word of God says and lives it. How does the diet cola can in the aquarium remind you of the person who obeys God's Word? When we obey God's Word, we could say that it keeps us afloat!

- Read 1 John 5:3-4.

- When something is "burdensome," as this verse says, what does that make you think of? Burdensome things weigh you down. They are heavy. They make you sink!

- When do you feel weighed down? What things are burdensome to you? (school work, family situations, friends, pressure to be the best at something, someone close to you is very ill)

- What can you do about that? How can God's Word help you? What steps can you take?

Other verses to use with this experiment:
- Deuteronomy 4:1
- Romans 2:6-8
- Colossians 3:22

Cola-rized Egg
Forgiveness

Scripture:

1 John 1:9 (ESV)

If we confess our sins, he is faithful and just to forgive us our sins and to cleanse us from all unrighteousness.

Lab Equipment

- cola
- damp cloth
- glass
- paper towel
- raw egg
- slatted spoon
- toothbrush
- toothpaste

Egg discolored by cola

Experiment

- Place a raw egg in a glass of cola. It should set in the cola for 3 or 4 hours.
- Use a slatted spoon to pull the egg from the cola. Pat it dry with a piece of paper towel. The egg is now stained brown.
- Put some toothpaste on a toothbrush. Scrub the shell of the egg, like you would brush your teeth.
- Wipe the toothpaste from the egg using a damp cloth.

Observation

- Describe the egg before you put it in the glass of cola.
- Describe the egg after setting in the cola for several hours.
- Describe the egg after you used the toothpaste and toothbrush on it.

- Was it easy or hard for the egg to get stained?
- Was it easy or hard for the egg to get clean?

Discussion

- Read 1 John 1:9.
- How do you connect the experiment with this scripture?
- Our egg had 3 stages: the way it started out, stained, and cleaned. Which of these stages is a picture of us when we are full of sin?
- What stained the egg? (cola)
- What stains our lives? (Sin, when we disobey God.)
- Was it difficult for us to get the egg stained? (No, it just sat in the cola. We are born with a sinful nature, and it isn't difficult for us to fall into a place or a situation where we sin.)
- Which stage of the egg looks like when we have been forgiven?
- How did the egg get cleaned up? (We used some toothpaste and a brush to clean it.) Was it difficult? (No. We did two small actions—put the toothpaste on the brush and did a little scrubbing.)
- Is it difficult for us to receive forgiveness from God? (No. It takes two actions—confessing our sin to Him and claiming Jesus' sacrifice as payment for our disobedience to God.)
- Which stage of the egg do you want to be like?

Other verses to use with this experiment:
- Psalm 103:10-12
- Isaiah 1:18
- Ephesians 4:31-32
- 1 Peter 4:8

Color Transfer
Serving

Scripture:

Matthew 25:35-40 (ESV)
"For I was hungry and you gave me food, I was thirsty and you gave me drink, I was a stranger and you welcomed me, I was naked and you clothed me, I was sick and you visited me, I was in prison and you came to me." Then the righteous will answer him, saying, "Lord, when did we see you hungry and feed you, or thirsty and give you drink? And when did we see you a stranger and welcome you, or naked and clothe you? And when did we see you sick or in prison and visit you?" And the King will answer them, "Truly, I say to you, as you did it to one of the least of these my brothers, you did it to me."

Lab Equipment

- 3 colors of food coloring
- 4 custard cups
- paper towel
- spoon
- water

Beginning

Experiment

- Fill 3 custard cups about two-thirds with water. Add 10 drops of one color of food coloring to each cup and stir. Rinse the spoon off in between stirring each color. Now, you should have 3 distinct and strong colors of water.

- Position the cups of colored water in a triangle and place the empty custard cup in the middle. The cups of colored water should each be about 3" from the empty one.

- Cut 3 strips of paper towel ½"-1" wide and about 6" long.

- Put one end of one of the strips of paper towel in the empty cup and the other end in one of the cups of colored water. Take a second strip and put one end in the empty cup and the other end in a different cup of colored water.

- Likewise, with the third strip, put one end in the empty cup and the other end in the last cup of colored water.
- Watch for a minute; then, let the cups sit for about 5 minutes.
- The colored water will move through the paper towel and fill what was an empty cup.

Observation

- How long did it take for the colored water to begin moving into the paper towel when it was placed in the cup?
- How far did the colored water move through the paper towel? Did it stop halfway?
- Describe what the custard cup in the center looked like at the beginning of the experiment.
- Describe what the custard cup in the center looked like after 5 minutes.
- Did we need exactly 3 cups of colored water for this to work?
- How many cups of colored water do you think we could've used?
- What did the water look like in the center custard cup after 5 minutes?
- What color was it?

Discussion

- Read Mark 25:35-40. How does this Scripture passage remind you of the experiment we just did? (Don't discount any ideas the kids may come up with and encourage them to think creatively and abstractly. You may even find that their direction is worth exploring or revisiting at another time.)
- Let's say the custard cup in the middle represents someone who has a need. Maybe this is someone who is poor and doesn't have enough money to rent a place for his family to live. All the cups of colored water represent Christ-followers who want to live as God wants them to live. What does this passage of scripture tell us we should do if we want to follow Christ? (We should help the person who is poor.)

- Thinking about this passage, what would the paper towel represent? (It reminds me of our hands reaching out, or when we somehow connect with the person who needs help...maybe talking with the person and finding out what is happening in his or her life.)

- Then, what would the colored water moving through the paper towel represent? (It's when we actually DO something. It's when we provide a way to help that person and put our words into action.)

- When we reach out to help and serve someone, it changes her. The custard cup in the middle was completely empty when we started. This person was hopeless and helpless. The care the people showed—the colored water custard cups—filled this person up. Her life changed. When we care for other people because we're grateful that God cares deeply about us, then they change. They're no longer empty, hopeless, and helpless. We are pouring God's love into them by serving them.

- Do you know someone who is hopeless right now? Someone who needs hope? Someone who needs help being filled up?

- Who can you reach out to this week? Name something you can do to pour God's love into someone else.

Other verses to use with this experiment:
- Romans 15:1
- Galatians 6:2
- Philippians 2:4

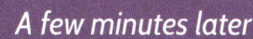

A few minutes later

Disappearing Eggshell
Life change

Scripture:

2 Corinthians 5:17 (ESV)

Therefore, if anyone is in Christ, he is a new creation. The old has passed away; behold, the new has come.

Lab Equipment

- clear glass
- raw egg
- vinegar
- water

Experiment

- Place a raw egg in a clear glass and fill the glass with vinegar.
- Set the glass aside for one day and don't touch it.
- On Day 2, pour off the vinegar completely and replace it with a fresh glass of vinegar. Make sure the egg is totally submerged.
- Leave it set...don't touch it...for 5 more days.
- Pour off the vinegar.
- Gently rinse the egg with water, lightly patting the foam off the outside.

Observation

- Describe what the egg looked like and felt like on Day 1 when you placed it in the glass of vinegar.
- Describe what the egg feels and looks like on Day 6.
- What has changed? What is missing?
- Where did the shell go?

- How is the egg on Day 6 like the raw egg we put in the glass on Day 1? How is it different from the raw egg?

Discussion

- Read 2 Corinthians 5:17.

- How does this experiment remind you of this verse?

- The verse talks about the "old" being gone. What "old" is gone from the egg? (The shell is gone.)

- When we confess our sins and ask Jesus to be our Savior, what "old" things are gone? (Our sins are gone. They've been stripped away, like the shell has been dissolved off the egg.)

- The verse talks about a "new creation." How is the egg a "new creation"? It's bigger than it was to begin with. It doesn't have a shell. It isn't runny now, but is soft and squishy.

- When we become believers in Jesus, how are we a "new creation"? (He doesn't just fix a piece of our lives, or put a Bandaid® on a hurt. No, He gives us a brand new start as if we had never sinned in the first place. We are brand new people!)

- When you become a follower of Christ, what changes in you? (attitude, worship, the way you treat others, what you do with your time)

Other verses to use with this experiment:
- Romans 12:2
- Philippians 3:21
- 1 John 3:2

Draw All Men
Drawn to Jesus

Scripture:

John 12:32-33 (ESV)

"And I, when I am lifted up from the earth, will draw all people to myself." He said this to show by what kind of death he was going to die.

Lab Equipment

- box of paper clips
- neodymium magnet*

Experiment

- Place half a box of paper clips in a pile on a flat surface.

- Some people have thick hands and others have long slender hands. Choose someone to assist you who has thin slender hands. He or she should place one hand over the pile of paper clips under the area where the finger joints are that join to the palm of the hand.

- Keeping the hand flat, lift it slowly. Nothing should happen.

- Now, place the neodymium magnet on the back of the hand, right on the center knuckles.

- Instruct the child to keep his or her hand flat and raise it slowly. All of the paper clips will hang from the palm of your volunteer's hand as she raises it.

- Make sure the person puts her hand back on the table before removing the magnet…or you'll have a big mess!

* A neodymium magnet can be purchased where you get science supplies. They are not expensive and are great to have in your toolbox of resources. Just watch out…if your toolbox is metal, you'll need some strong arms to pull the magnet away!

Observation

- What happened when our volunteer's hand raised without the magnet on the back of the hand?
- How many of the paper clips stuck to the bottom of the person's hand when the neodymium magnet was used? What was your reaction when all the paper clips were picked up?
- How many paper clips did you think the magnet could handle?
- What caused the paper clips to be lifted up?
- If we laid paper clips around the edge of the person's hand, would they be picked up?
- What would happen if we pulled the magnet away from their hand?

Discussion

- Read John 12:32-33.
- What are these verses talking about when they say "lifted up"? (Jesus was lifted up on the cross; He was crucified.)
- How do you relate our experiment to these verses?
- What do you think the paper clips represent? (People. The paper clips under the hand are people who are covered by Jesus—who believe in Jesus as their Savior and Lord.)
- What happens to paper clips that are not covered by the hand? (They are not raised by the magnet.) What happens to people who do not claim Jesus as their Savior? (They won't live forever with Him.)
- When our volunteer lifted her hand without the magnet on her knuckles, nothing happened. On our own, we can't get back to God. Each person has disobeyed, and because of that, has been separated from God. We can't be lifted to God on our own. We don't have that kind of power.
- The magnet represents Jesus. How was Jesus raised? He was raised up on the

cross. He was raised out of the grave. He was raised up as He ascended into heaven. It is because of His sacrifice on the cross, because He beat Satan's hold on Him through death, and because He has gone to prepare a place for us...that we can be drawn to Him and be raised also.

- Jesus paid for our disobedience when He went to the cross. His power overcame the grave. God accepts Jesus' sacrifice for us when we believe that He is God's Son and has that power. Now, we can be lifted up with Him.

- What has the power in this experiment? The paper clips or the magnet? If we are the paper clips, then how much power do we have to get ourselves to heaven? (None without Jesus.)

- What has to happen for God to accept us again—to forgive us for turning our backs on Him through our disobedience? Once we admit our sin, and believe that Jesus is God's Son and our personal sacrifice, we are brought back to a relationship with God. We are lifted up! We can enjoy God's company again! Just like the magnet had the power to lift up all those paper clips, Jesus has the power to bring everyone back to God, if they will only believe.

- Is Jesus' power to bring us back to God just for one or two people? (No, it's for everyone! We picked up lots of paper clips, not just one or two.)

- Repeat John 12:32 again slowly, together.

Other verses to use with this experiment:
- Psalm 145:18
- John 6:44

Dropping Hex Nuts
Rescue

Scripture:

2 Timothy 4:18 (ESV)
The Lord will rescue me from every evil deed and bring me safely into his heavenly kingdom. To him be the glory forever and ever. Amen.

Lab Equipment

- 30" piece of string
- 15 hex nuts (1/4" hole)

Experiment

- Tie one hex nut to the end of a piece of string that is approximately 30" in length.

- On the other end of the string, thread 14 hex nuts. Loop the end of the string around and tie it, so you have a loop of hex nuts.

- Trim off any excess string from both ends where you have tied knots.

- Hold an index finger out straight and hang the string over this finger.

- Pull the single hex nut so that the string is pulled at a 90-degree angle from

the string hanging over your finger. As you pull on this single hex nut, the loop of 14 will rise toward the index finger.

- Pull the string parallel to the floor, so the loop of hex nuts are only hanging down about 3" from your index finger.
- Let go of the single hex nut that you're holding. Keep your index finger steady. The single hex nut will swing around the index finger several times and keep the loop from falling to the ground.

Observation

- What did you expect to happen when you let go of the one hex nut?
- What was pulling on the string?
- How was the one hex nut able to stop the 14 from falling?

Discussion

- Read 2 Timothy 4:18.
- How does the experiment remind you of this verse?
- We didn't expect the single hex nut to catch the 14 that were dropping so fast. Our One True God can rescue us when life gets out of control—when things seem to be going downhill fast, and there's lots going wrong.
- What was your reaction the first time the single hex nut stopped the others from falling? Did you say "Wow"? Or giggle? Or oooh and aaah? What does this verse say our reaction should be when God rescues us? We should give Him glory. How do we do that? We need to oooh and aaah both privately and publicly, letting others know what God is up to!
- Have you ever felt like God rescued you when you were in a bad situation? How has He kept you from falling?

Other verses to use with this experiment:
- Psalm 71:2
- Psalm 140:1
- Isaiah 41:10

Egg in a Bottle
Drawn Near to God

Scripture:

Galatians 5:24 (ESV)
And those who belong to Christ Jesus have crucified the flesh with its passions and desires.

Lab Equipment

- 3 birthday candles
- hard-boiled egg
- large-mouthed bottle (1.5" opening, like a Frappucino)
- matches
- paper

Experiment

- Remove the shell from a hard-boiled egg.

- Poke 3 birthday candles into the smaller end of the hard-boiled egg. The candles need to be fairly close together, because they will need to go into the mouth of the bottle during the experiment.

- Light the candles.

- Hold a large-mouthed bottle upside down. Frappucino bottles work great, but an iced tea bottle is too small of an opening. You need an opening of 1.5".

- Move the egg close to the mouth of the bottle and insert the birthday candles into the bottle. Do not touch the egg to the bottle.

- Let the flames from the candles warm the inside of the bottle. Then, move the egg closer so that it is touching the mouth of the bottle. Hold it gently.

- Once the egg is against the opening to the bottle, the flames will use up the oxygen inside the bottle and they will go out. That's when the cool stuff happens! The egg will squeeze up into the bottle...without any pushing at all.

Observation

- Where did the egg need to be in order to be ready to go in the bottle?
- What happened when the egg was brought close to the mouth of the bottle and touched it?
- What had to happen to the candles before the egg would go inside the bottle?

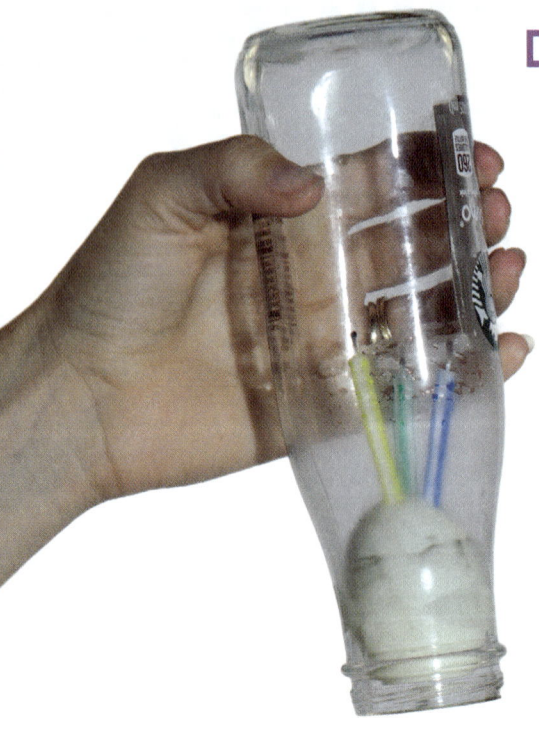

Discussion

- Read James 4:8.
- How does this verse and experiment connect in your mind?
- When you learn something about God, does that pull you toward Him or push you away? (The more I know about God, the more I am drawn to Him and want to find out more.)
- The candles had to go out in order for the egg to enter the bottle. If you belong to Christ, what "goes out"–what dies? The sinful things we wanted to do are snuffed out. When we live close to Jesus, we want to live like He wants us to, and there's no place for those sinful things to exist. Sin and God cannot live together. You have to choose one or the other!
- When we accept Jesus as Savior, the sin is snuffed out, and we are drawn close to God.
- When do you feel especially close to God? When do you feel Him drawing you to Him?

Other verses to use with this experiment:
- Acts 17:27
- James 4:8

And now, for getting that egg OUT of the bottle!

Hold the bottle slightly tilted in the air and blow into it...really hard. Blow down the side of the egg. Keep blowing. Yes, believe it or not, the egg just came out!

Egg Prints
Love

Scripture:

John 13:35 (ESV)

By this all people will know that you are my disciples, if you have love for one another.

Lab Equipment

- boiled eggs
- cup
- egg-coloring kit
- old pantyhose
- paper towel
- scissors
- small leaves
- water

Experiment

- Boil some eggs.

- Prepare cups of egg-coloring dye (same as that for Easter eggs).

- Press a small leaf against the egg, smoothing it out completely. Get the wrinkles out as the leaf curves against the egg.

- Carefully, place the egg into the toe of a pair of pantyhose, making sure that the leaf does not move or the edges do not get curled up.

- Pull the pantyhose around the egg snugly, and then tie a knot as close to the egg as possible.

- You can cut some of the remaining pantyhose away, but leave enough so you can hold onto it. Hold onto this excess and ease the egg down into the cup of dye. Leave it there for a while, so the egg takes on a deep color.

- Pull the egg out of the cup of dye and carefully remove the pantyhose.

- Pat the egg dry with some paper towel.

- Slip your fingernail under the edge of the leaf and slowly lift it away from the egg. The egg should be white where the leaf was laying against it.

Observation

- What did the egg look like before we put it in the dye?
- Why couldn't the dye color all of the egg?
- How long did it take to dye the egg?
- What did you notice first when you look at the completed egg?
- Close your eyes and describe the egg.

Discussion

- Read John 13:35.
- According to this verse, how will people know we are Christ-followers?
- How does this verse remind you of our experiment with the egg and the leaf?
- If we put this egg that has the leaf impression on it in a full carton of eggs that have all been dyed the same color, how easy would it be to find the egg we used in this experiment? Why would it be so easy?
- What do you know about a girl who is wearing a Girl Scout sash? What do you know about a man who is wearing a Dodgers' T-shirt? What do you know about a woman who has a bookcase full of bowling trophies? The sash, the T-shirt, and the trophies are ways we know more about the person: that person is a Girl Scout, he likes the Dodgers, and she is a good bowler. These things tell us what is important to them. As Christians, how will people know what is important to us?
- It should be easy for people to recognize us as Christians because our love is so obvious! We don't need to wear a T-shirt that says, "I love you because I follow Jesus." Our actions of love should communicate that.

- When have you shown someone love? How could you make a "love impression" on someone today?

Alternate Discussion

- Let's think of the egg as someone who doesn't know God ... maybe someone who needs help and doesn't know what to do. When we do something to demonstrate love to that person who needs help, that leaves an impression on them, which reminds me of the leaf that left an impression on the egg. They will remember it. They will remember your act of love. When we placed the egg in the cup, we covered it with the dye. When we reach out to someone who needs help, we are covering them with love. They will never be the same.

- We can be nice to someone, but when we love in extraordinary ways because God loved us in an extraordinary way by sending His Son Jesus, then people connect our act of love to our being a follower of Jesus. Their lives are changed because we covered them with God's love!

- When have you seen someone show extraordinary love to someone else? What kind of impression did it leave on you?

Other verses to use with this experiment:
- John 13:15
- Colossians 3:12-15
- 1 Peter 4:8
- 1 John 4:7-8

Eggs-traordinary Strength
God's Promises

Scripture:

2 Corinthians 1:20
For all the promises of God find their Yes in him. That is why it is through him that we utter our Amen to God for his glory.

Lab Equipment

- 4 uncooked eggs
- a medium-thick book
- a permanent marker
- a thin book
- egg carton
- scissors or box cutter
- very large heavy book

Experiment

- Using a pair of scissors or a box cutter, cut the top off an egg carton. You will only be using the bottom section for this experiment.

- Place 4 eggs in the carton, with the smaller pointy end of the egg down. Place 2 eggs near each end, leaving the 2 very end wells on each side vacant.

- Find the largest, thickest book possible, and then two smaller books. Ask the kids to guess which of the books the eggs can hold without breaking. Make it very dramatic, and play up the mess that could possibly be made.

- Set the thinnest book on top of the eggs, positioning the eggs equal distance from each end of the book. As you put the book in place—and, by the way, put it on gently—try to get it centered over the eggs as well as possible. Once you demonstrate that the eggs will hold the thin book, remove the book.

- Set the medium-sized book on top of the eggs in the same manner. Once you see that the eggs will hold this book, remove it.

- Now that you've witnessed the eggs were able to support both the small and medium-sized books, with a dramatic flare, set the large book on top of the eggs.

Observation

- When buying eggs at the store, what do you always do before you put them in your grocery cart? (You check to make sure none are broken.)

- How many eggs did we need for the experiment? How were the eggs placed?

- Which of the books did you think the eggs would be able to support without breaking? Did it surprise you that we could put so much weight on the eggs?

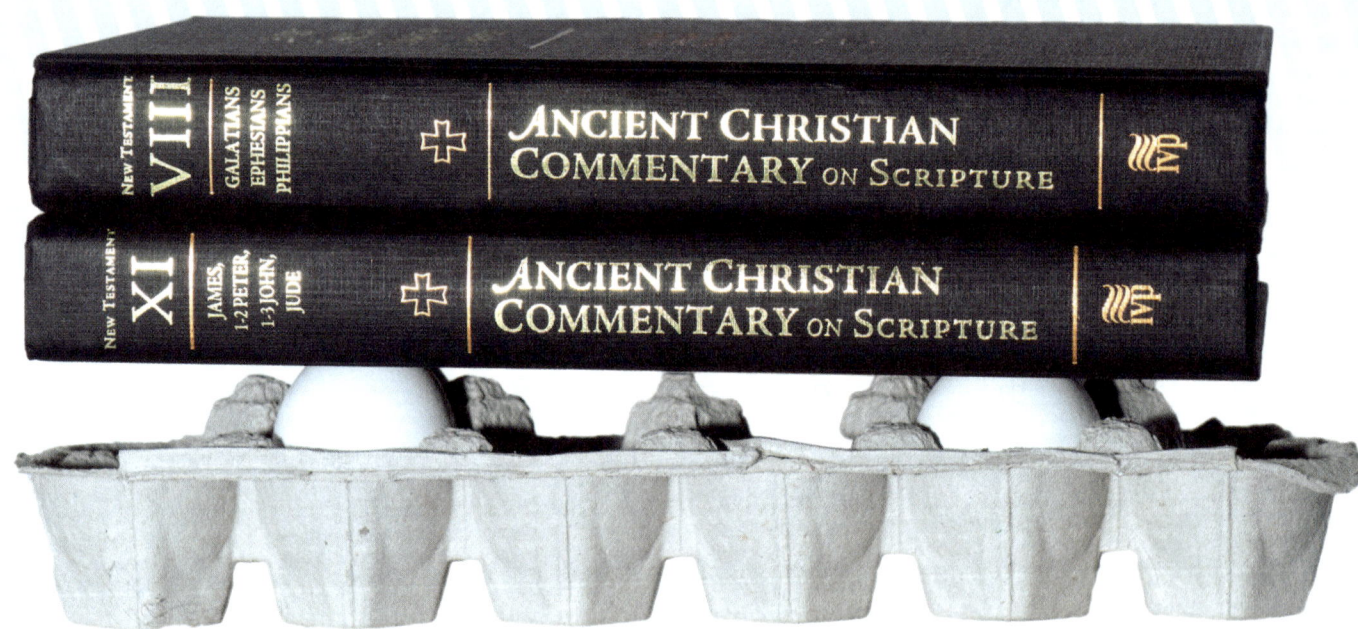

Discussion

- Read 2 Peter 1:4.

- In this verse, what are precious and great? (God's promises!)

- Just like we doubted that the eggs could support that big book, sometimes we think our problems are too big for God to handle. But, God gave us many promises. We can believe them. We can stand on them. We can put our heavy problems on His promises. None of our problems will crush God.

- Name some of the promises of God.

    - He promises to never leave us.
    - He promises to love us.
    - He promises that nothing will separate us from Him.
    - He promises to give us new life when we believe in Jesus.
    - He promises us heaven when we believe in Him.
    - He promises to give us new strength when we feel weak.
    - One thing God promises NOT to do is to break His promises!

- Write the promises of God on the eggs with the permanent marker. Then, place the book on top of them again. This book represents YOU, and you can rest...you can stand...you can depend on God!

- Is there a promise of God you have a difficult time believing? Pray that God will help you believe in that promise.

- A little extra...Play the song by Sanctus Real called "Hold On to the Promises." Encourage the kids to share the phrases that really stuck out to them in this song.

Other verses to use with this experiment:
- Psalm 119:133
- Hebrews 10:23

Elephant Toothpaste
Praise

Scripture:

Psalm 119:171 (NIV)

May my lips overflow with praise, for you teach me your decrees.

Lab Equipment

- ½ cup of 30-volume hydrogen peroxide liquid*
- 1 packet of dry yeast
- 3 T. lukewarm water
- condiment cup
- food coloring
- Ivory liquid dish soap
- large tray with a lip
- paper towel
- spoon
- tall, clear glass cylinder

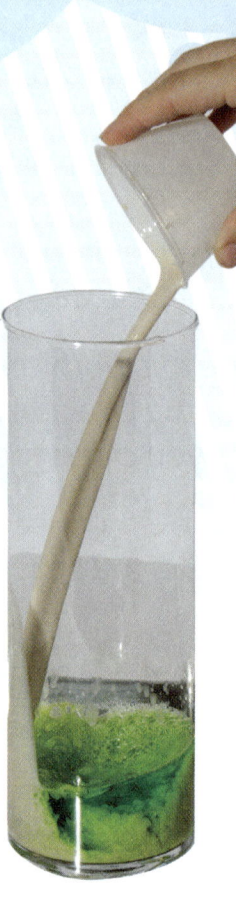

Experiment

- Right before you start, put the envelope of yeast in the condiment cup. Add 3 T. of lukewarm water and stir. It will lump a little. Get most of the lumps out and then let it set while you prepare the rest of the experiment. It needs to set at least 3 minutes.

- Place the glass cylinder on a large tray (to catch any mess).

- Pour ½ cup of hydrogen peroxide into the cylinder.

- Add a few drops of food coloring and 2 T of Ivory liquid dish soap.

- Swirl these around in the cylinder so they are mixed well.

- In one quick motion, pour the yeast/water into the cylinder and step back.

* The hydrogen peroxide is inexpensive and available at beauty supply stores. Do not get the cream form. This is NOT the hydrogen peroxide you use on cuts.

Observation

- Ooooh! Aaaah! It just keeps coming!

- Describe what's happening and what it looks like.

- What had to happen for the foam to form and start overflowing? (We had to add the yeast.)

- Other than seeing the foam flow out of the container, is there a smell? Is there heat? Don't touch the foam, but place your hand close to it and you can feel the heat coming off of it.

Discussion

- Read Psalm 119:171.

- How do you connect this verse with the experiment we just did?

- This verse says that we will overflow with praise when we know God's commands. When we experience God and live according to His Word, then praise comes out of our lives. God wants us to be generous. When we decide to be generous and take action, we realize that God is praised through our generosity. When we extend forgiveness to others, like God tells us to do, we offer our praises. When we are content with what we have and do not want what others have—as God commanded—we can praise, instead of being jealous or covetous. What other decrees can we keep that will bring God praise? Praise just keeps coming—it overflows—as we stay in God's will!

- Adding yeast was a decision we made. We didn't have to. The mixture in the cylinder could've stayed just like it was—calm and unnoticeable. Praising God with your life is also a choice. Each time you decide to follow one of God's commands, then He is praised.

- Does your life overflow with praise to God?

- What can you do that will make it obvious that you praise God in everything?

Other verses to use with this experiment:
- Psalm 119:133
- Hebrews 10:23

Energy Stick
Sharing the Gospel

Scripture:

1 Corinthians 15:3 (ESV)

For I delivered to you as of first importance what I also received: that Christ died for our sins in accordance with the Scriptures.

Lab Equipment

- Energy Stick*

* Energy Sticks can be purchased at science supply websites for $10-$15, and at tinahouser.net.

Experiment

- Hold the Energy Stick in one hand, making sure your hand is in contact with the metal band at one end of the stick.

- With the other hand, take hold of the metal band at the other end of the stick. The Energy Stick will light up and make a funny, "techy" noise.

- Choose someone to join you. You will hold one end of the Energy Stick and your partner will hold the other end. Now, hold hands with this person and the Energy Stick will light up and make the sound. The kids will be absolutely delighted when the tiny green and purple lights in the tube light up.

- Add more people to the circle. Everyone should be holding hands, with one person holding one end of the stick and another person holding the other end.

- Choose two people standing next to each other to stop holding hands. Hold hands. Don't hold hands. The Energy Stick will lose its connection each time the two people separate their hands.

Observation

- What happened to the Energy Stick when the single person touched both ends?

- What happened when everyone kept holding hands?
- What happened when one person dropped his or her hand?

Discussion

- Read 1 Corinthians 15:3.

- What comes to mind when you think about this verse and the experiment with the Energy Stick?

- It is an awesome experience to be the special person who gets to help someone meet Jesus. Your words may be what they need. You may be the one who helps them "make the connection." Sometimes, it only takes one time talking with someone and they are ready to make that decision.

- How do you know when someone is ready to make a decision for Christ? You don't! Only God knows that. You don't know whether or not it is their special moment. You don't know how the Holy Spirit has been working with them. But, each of us has the responsibility as Christians to take advantage of those times when people are asking questions. When someone asks a question about your faith, it's a signal that he or she are thinking about God.

- Do you always feel like sharing how God can change someone's life?

Do you ever question whether or not you should? What if that is the moment when that person wants to ask God to forgive her and change her life?

- Most of the time, it takes many people speaking God's truth and showing God's love before someone makes that life-changing decision. We make excuses, though, about why we shouldn't be one of the people speaking truth and love. What kind of excuses do we make? "Oh, I just don't feel like it." "I'm not sure I'll say the right thing." "They'll just think I'm weird." "I don't really have time right now to have a long talk."

When someone doesn't take advantage of the opportunity, there is disconnect. That may be the time when the person was going to make a decision. Don't step away! Step INTO every chance to speak up for God. It just might be the moment when that person makes the connection. Each time someone stepped away, dropped his hand, or didn't hold on to the Energy Stick, the connection was broken. So, the next time you're thinking of an excuse not to talk about Jesus, remember the Energy Stick...and grab hold of the opportunity!

For those of you who teach children, don't step away from any opportunity. Don't allow yourself to make an excuse as to why you can't teach today or why it's not a good time for you. It may be the connecting moment for that child!

Other verses to use with this experiment:
- Psalm 145:4
- Luke 24:47
- Romans 8:17
- Philemon 1:6

Floating Ms
God Doesn't See Labels

Scripture:

Galatians 3:26-28 (ESV)
For in Christ Jesus you are all sons of God, through faith. For as many of you as were baptized into Christ have put on Christ. There is neither Jew nor Greek, there is neither slave nor free, there is no male and female, for you are all one in Christ Jesus.

Lab Equipment

- M&Ms™
- small bowl
- warm water

Experiment

- Place one of each color M&M™ in the bottom of a bowl, with the M side up.
- Gently add warm water to the side of the bowl until the M&Ms™ are completely covered. Don't pour the water directly on top of the candies.
- Wait 3-5 minutes.
- DO NOT stir the water at any time. Just let the M&Ms™ set.

Observation

- What changes do you notice to the candies?
- What changes do you notice to the outer coating? The color of the water?
- Can you tell which M&M™ was red? blue? yellow? green?

- What is gone from the M&M™?
- Did the Ms come off intact, or were some of them in parts?

Discussion

- Read Galatians 3:26-28.

- When you read this verse, what connects with the experiment we just did?

- The scripture talks about some labels that people had at that time: male and female, Jew and Greek, slave and free. What labels do we give people today? (Smart, poor, shy, pushy, leader, follower, slow, athlete, emotional, uncoordinated.) We all have characteristics that make us different than other people, but God just sees us as people He loves.

- When God looks at people, does He see their label(s)? God sees us all as His people—nothing more, nothing less. We're all the same in one main way: We all need to be forgiven and brought back to Him. The labels have come off in His sight, and we all appear the same—people in need of a Savior.

- Are there some people you think are worthy to talk to about God and others you don't want to talk to about Him? Why do you feel that way?

- What action(s) can you take to see people the way that God sees them? How can you lift off the label and see past it?

Other verses to use with this experiment:
- Acts 10:34
- 1 John 3:1
- 1 John 4:7-8

Floating Paper Clip
Advice

Scripture:

1 Corinthians 11:1 (ESV)
Be imitators of me, as I am of Christ.

Lab Equipment

- bowl
- paper clip
- piece of paper towel
- water

Paper Clip Sinks

Experiment

- Fill the bowl with water.
- Drop a paper clip into the bowl and watch it sink.
- Now, place a 2" x 2" square of paper towel on the surface of the water. Lay the paper clip on top of the paper towel.
- The paper towel will soak up the water and then sink in the bowl, but will leave the paper clip floating on the surface of the water.

Observation

- What was the difference between the two times we put the paper clip in the bowl?
- Why do you think the paper clip sunk the first time but floated the second time?

Paper Clip Supported by Towel

Discussion

- Read 1 Corinthians 11:1.

- How do you relate this scripture to the paper clip experiment?

- Have you ever tried something on your own and really flopped at it?

- The piece of paper towel supported the paper clip for a while. We need to find people who will support us until we're ready to stand on our own (or float on our own). When has someone supported you as you learned a new task–until you got it?

Now It Floats!

- The paper clip needed some help to be able to float. Then, it was fine. As you try to live for Jesus, sometimes you won't know how or what to do. What should you do then? You need to find godly people you trust, who follow what God wants them to do; then model yourself after them. Imitate them. If they are godly people, they are already imitating Christ.

- When have you not known how to handle a situation and asked for someone's help? How did their advice help you?

- Sometimes we all need someone else's support and advice. We want to float; we don't want to sink! Make sure you choose the right people to give you that help and advice, though. What kind of people should we imitate? We need to find people who want to be like Christ–whose desire it is to make God happy. We can see how God wants us to live when we watch them. Those are the people we try to be like–imitate people who are imitating Christ!

- Name 3 people you can imitate with confidence, who are living lives that imitate Christ. When you wonder how you should react to a situation, you can imagine what that person would do, or you could actually ask their advice.

- Can you be one of the people others imitate? (Of course, you can!) What characteristics, habits, and attitudes should you work on to be a godly person that others want to imitate? (You need to imitate Christ, and then others will want to imitate you!)

Other verses to use with this experiment:
- Proverbs 13:20
- Hebrews 13:7
- 1 Peter 5:1-5

Fuzzy Magnet
Individual Gifts

Scripture:

Ephesians 4:11 (NASB)

And He gave some as apostles, and some as prophets, and some as evangelists, and some as pastors and teachers.

Lab Equipment

- bar magnets
- chenille sticks
- empty 2-liter bottle
- scissors or paper cutter

Experiment

- You will need a bunch of chenille sticks of different colors. This is a great use for the leftovers from crafts. Cut these into short pieces, about ½" – 1" in length.

- A paper cutter makes this a quick task because you can do a handful at a time and push them through with each chop. Please don't bother to measure the pieces!

- Place all the chenille pieces in the empty 2-liter bottle and cap it. You'll want at least 2" of fuzzy pieces at the bottom of the bottle.

- Give 3 or 4 kids a bar magnet. They will gather around the bottle and choose a spot where they will lay their magnet against the bottle outside the fuzzy pieces.

- The kids will keep their magnet bar against the bottle and drag it up the bottle. Different color fuzzy pieces of chenille stubs will follow their magnet.

Observation

- Describe what the 2-liter bottle of chenille stubs looked like when we started.
- Were all the chenille stubs alike? How were they different from one another?
- What happened when we drug the magnets up the bottle?
- What do you think would've happened to the chenille stubs if you had pulled the magnet away from the bottle?

Discussion

- Read Ephesians 4:11.
- Discuss how what happened in the experiment relates to this verse.
- As each magnet was pulled up the side of the bottle, there was a group of chenille stubs that stuck to it. The chenille stubs that stuck to that particular magnet were different colors and different lengths. Some of the magnets had larger groups of chenille stubs stuck to them.
- The pieces that stuck to one magnet were all different, but they were all alike in one way—they were stuck to the same magnet! This verse says that God calls some people to be pastors. Pastors don't all look alike. Some are short. Some are tall. Some have dark skin, and others have white skin or yellow skin. They don't all speak the same language. They don't all live in the same place. They are all different, but they have one thing in common: God has called them to be pastors.
- Are there more chenille stubs stuck to one magnet than to another one? Do you think there are equal numbers of pastors as there are teachers? Are there equal numbers of prophets as evangelists? Each one, though, no matter how clumped together, shares a common calling. They have one thing in common. They are stuck on the one thing that God called them to do!

- Do any of the groups or magnets look more important? Nope! When God calls someone to be a pastor or a teacher or a prophet...or whatever He is calling YOU to do...that doesn't mean your calling is any more important or any less important than anyone else's. Each one is serving just as God desires.

Other verses to use with this experiment:
- Romans 12:3-8
- 1 Corinthians 7:17

Boiling Mad
Anger

Scripture:

Acts 19:28 (ESV)
When they heard this they were enraged and were crying out, "Great is Artemis of the Ephesians!"

Lab Equipment

- hand boilers (These can be purchased from a science equipment supplier, such as stevespanglerscience.com, for about $5.00 each.)

Experiment

- Have several people do this simultaneously, so you'll need several hand boilers. Each person will hold a hand boiler by the tip, letting it hang freely. They may want to cup their other hand under it, just in case their grip slips, but DO NOT touch the hand boiler at this point other than at the very tip top.

- At the signal, each person will gently wrap both hands around the bottom bulb of the hand boiler.

- They will continue to hold onto the bottom bulb until all hand boilers are boiling. It will take only a few seconds.
- Once the liquid in the hand boiler comes up the tube and appears to be boiling, then signal everyone to go back to suspending the hand boiler by holding it by the tip.

Observation

- Where was the colored liquid when you began?
- What happened when you wrapped your hands around the bottom bulb? Describe how the liquid moved through the hand boiler.
- What made the liquid go back down into the bottom bulb after it had been "boiling"?
- Did all the hand boilers start boiling at the same time?
- What do you think caused them to boil at different times?

Discussion

- Read Acts 19:24-28.
- How can you connect this scripture with this experiment?
- We sometimes describe someone who is really, really angry as being "boiling mad." Who was boiling mad in this passage? (The business people of Ephesus were angry and started shouting.) They were shouting in anger. Do you ever shout when you get angry?
- Why were the business people in Ephesus mad? (When people started believing in Jesus, the new believers didn't buy the silver souvenir statues of all the other gods—the made-up gods. The silversmiths, especially, were upset because it was taking away one of the main ways they made money. When people started believing in Jesus, it hurt their businesses big time!)
- For what reasons do people get boiling mad?

- We could get the liquid to settle down by holding it differently—by the tip. What can you do to calm down when you're really mad?

- Some things aren't important enough to get angry about. Name some things you (or someone else) get angry about that really aren't worth the hassle.

- Other things are really wrong, and unless people get upset about what's happening, nothing will change. Name some things you (or someone else) need to get angry about (poverty, slavery, lying, deceitfulness, bullying, hunger, etc.)

Other verses to use with this experiment:
- Daniel 3:19
- Proverbs 19:11
- Ecclesiastes 7:9
- Ephesians 4:31

He's Not Here!
Jesus' resurrection

Scripture:

Matthew 28:6 (ESV)

He is not here, for he has risen, as he said. Come, see the place where he lay.

Lab Equipment

- biodegradable packing peanut (Biodegradable packing peanuts can be purchased at hobby stores, or you can get them FREE from a Mary Kay Cosmetics distributor. All of their products are shipped in these biodegradable peanuts...and the salespeople have loads of them!)
- jar with a tight lid
- water

Experiment

- Fill a jar about two-thirds with water.
- Add a biodegradable packing peanut.
- Secure the lid.
- Shake vigorously as you count to 3, slowly.

Observation

- What did you place in the jar of water?
- What did we do to the jar after it was sealed?
- After shaking to the count of 3, what did you see in the water?
- Where did the packing peanut go?

Discussion

- Do the experiment again, but with some dialogue as you go through this time. Indicate that the jar represents the grave. *The packing peanut is Jesus. They put Jesus in the grave and rolled the stone across the entrance to seal the tomb.* Snap on the lid of the jar. *He was in the grave for 3 days. Count with me...1...2...3.* While you count, shake the jar vigorously for each day. *On the third day, the women went to the grave and what did they discover? What do you see in our jar? We can look for the packing peanut, but it's gone! The women looked for Jesus, but the angels told them that He was not there. He had risen!*

- *What did you think when you first realized that the packing peanut was not in the jar?*

- *Let's imagine for just a moment what the women first thought when they saw the stone had been moved and Jesus wasn't there.* What do you think was going through their minds?

- *How do you think they felt AFTER hearing what the angel had to say?*

- *How did the fact that Jesus was NOT in the grave change things?*

Additional Lesson

Matthew 25:14-30
You could also use this experiment with the story of the talents to represent the man who buried his talent (put it in the jar). He had it taken away when the master returned to find out how he had neglected to use it (packing peanut gone).

High Bouncer
God's ways

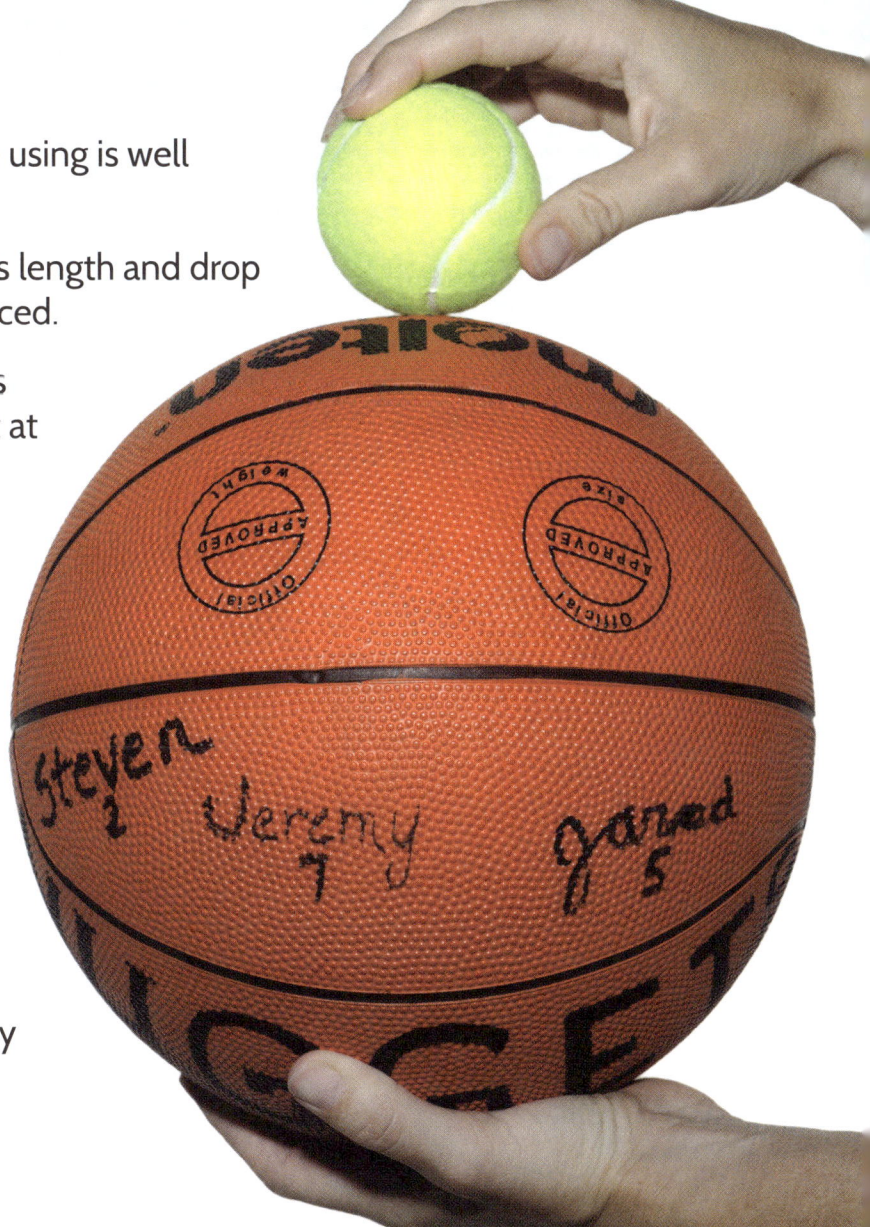

Scripture:

Isaiah 55:9 (ESV)

For as the heavens are higher than the earth, so are my ways higher than your ways and my thoughts than your thoughts.

Lab Equipment

- basketball
- tennis ball

Experiment

- Make sure the basketball you're using is well inflated.
- Hold the tennis ball out at arm's length and drop it. Note how high the ball bounced.
- Hold the basketball out at arm's length. Hold the tennis ball out at arm's length, but resting at the very top of the basketball.
- At the same moment, drop both balls.
- The tennis ball will bounce back much higher than expected.

Observation

- How high did the tennis ball bounce when it was dropped by itself?

- How high did the basketball bounce?
- How high did the tennis ball bounce when it was dropped with the basketball?

Discussion

- Read Isaiah 55:9. How does this verse remind you of the experiment we did with the two balls?

- Before we turn our lives over to God, we think of Him the way the tennis ball bounced the first time. "Okay...whatever...God probably has power. I'm not that excited about God."

- When we become God-followers and get to know God through His Word, prayer, and worship, we understand that He is much bigger and more powerful than we ever thought. His ways are much higher than what we imagined! The second time the tennis ball bounced higher than we thought it would. Weren't you amazed at that? The more we get to know God, the more He amazes us by the way He works!

- As you get to know God, He constantly shows you how His ways are higher. What does it mean, "His ways are higher?" He has answers to questions we thought had no answers. He loves people we thought no one could love. He has the power to heal when we think there's no way to get beyond a sickness.

Other verses to use with this experiment:
- Isaiah 6:1
- Isaiah 57:15

Hovering Bottle
Jesus' Birth

Scripture:

Matthew 2:9 (NIV)

After they had heard the king, they went on their way, and the star they had seen when it rose went ahead of them until it stopped over the place where the child was.

Lab Equipment

- 2-liter bottle (full)
- bottle balancer (available from teachersource.com for about $10)
- clean flat surface

Experiment

- Set the angled end of the balance board against the table.

- Insert the neck of a 2-liter bottle through the hole in the board.

- Check to make sure the angled end of the board is resting against the table completely.

- You will be able to feel when the 2-liter bottle is balanced. Gently release it and the bottle will be suspended in midair. If it doesn't seem to want to balance, then your surface is not completely flat. The lightweight plastic tables frequently pose a problem, because their surface is a little wavy. If the bottle wants to tilt one direction, then raise that end of the surface a little by adding some folded paper.

Observation

- Describe what the bottle is doing.

- Would you feel comfortable setting something breakable (like a china tea cup) under the bottle? Why or why not?

- Why is this amazing? (Bottles aren't supposed to hang in the air like this.)

Discussion

- Read Matthew 2:9.

- How does this verse remind you of the hovering bottle?

- Tape a construction paper star on the end of the bottle. Point to the table under the star. What did the wise men find here?

- This is pretty unusual to see a bottle hanging in the air like this. Why do you think the wise men were following the star? What was so unusual about it?

- Why do you think God used a star to "hover" over where the young Jesus was?

- Most of the time, our nativity sets show that the wise men came to the manger, but they actually came later than that. Mary and Joseph and the little boy Jesus were living in a house by the time the wise men arrived. How do we know that from reading the scriptures? Check out verse 11.

- Do you think anyone else, besides the wise men, realized the star was hovering over the house where Jesus was?

Other verses to use with this experiment:
- Genesis 1:2
- Isaiah 31:5

Hovering Ping-Pong Ball
Witnessing

Scripture:

Acts 1:8 (ESV)

But you will receive power when the Holy Spirit has come upon you, and you will be my witnesses in Jerusalem and in all Judea and Samaria, and to the end of the earth.

Lab Equipment

- blow dryer
- gift wrap tube
- paper towel tube
- ping-pong ball®
- toilet paper tube

Experiment

- Before beginning, test to make sure your ping-pong ball® will easily go through the toilet paper, paper towel, and giftwrap tubes.

- Ping-pong balls® can vary slightly in size and weight, and believe it or not, that slight difference will change how the experiment goes.

- Use one hand to hold the blow dryer with the nozzle pointing up. Turn it on. You'll need to experiment with the setting you use and the ball, according to the power of your blow dryer and the weight of the ball.

- With the other hand, gently place the ping-pong ball® in the airstream above the nozzle and release the ball. It should dance a little but will hover there.

- Now, hold a toilet paper tube so that the tube is vertical and is parallel to the airstream. Move the tube over the ping-pong ball® and then slowly bring it closer and closer to the ball. When the tube gets almost close enough to touch the ball, the ball will move through the tube. On mine, using the lighter weight white ball on a low setting moved the ball through the tube to rest

right above the end of the toilet paper tube. If I use the red ball (a little heavier) and put the blow dryer on high, the ball will shoot through the tube. Choose the power setting you are going to use beforehand, and keep that same setting throughout.

- Do the same thing with the paper towel tube.
- And lastly, do the same thing with the gift wrap tube.

Observation

- What caused the ping-pong ball® to move through the tubes?
- Does the ball always land in the same place?
- Did we change the power of the blow dryer to make the ball go through the longer tube?
- What provides the power for the ball to shoot through the tubes?
- What is the one thing we have to do to start everything in motion? (Turn on the blow dryer!)

Discussion

- What stayed the same no matter what tube we used? (The power on the blow dryer stayed the same, but the ball shot further depending on the length of the tube.)
- Read Acts 1:8. How does this experiment remind you of this verse?
- How is this like the Holy Spirit empowering people to do His work? (Some people spread the Good News of Jesus in their neighborhood and city. They stay close at home, but still the Holy Spirit uses them.) Which tube are they like? Some people go further away from home to share about Jesus? Which tube are they like? And, some people travel to the other side of the world to be missionaries. Which tube are they like? They are sent far!

We did all of those with the blow dryer set on the same power setting. All those people are empowered by the same Holy Spirit. There's not a little

Holy Spirit and a high-powered Holy Spirit. It's the same Spirit, but He gives each of us a different mission field.

- The only thing we have to do is to make ourselves available for the Holy Spirit. When we placed the ping-pong ball® in the airstream of the blow dryer, we made the ball available to have awesome things done to it. None of that could happen until the ball was in the airstream. How is that like being used by God?

Other verse to use with this experiment:
- John 17:18

On and On
Don't continue to sin

Scripture:

1 John 5:18 (ESV)
We know that everyone who has been born of God does not keep on sinning....

Lab Equipment

- can of inertia beads (Inertia beads [or Newton's beads] can be purchased at **stevespanglerscience.com** for about $15.)

Experiment

- Thread the inertia beads into the can as instructed on the package. If you have carried the beads around a lot since putting them in the can, it would be best to rethread them.

- A 2"-3" length of the inertia beads should be hanging off the top edge of the can. On this particular set, the end beads are red, while the rest of the beads are blue. Set the can on a table, preferably chest high, where it can be seen and you can get a good pull on the beads.

- Grab the end of the string of beads and then quickly yank down. As soon as you yank, let go of the beads.

Observation

- What amazed you about the beads?

- What happened to the beads?

- Did you have to help the beads for them to continue to come out of the can?
- How could you have stopped the beads from coming out?

Discussion

- Read 1 John 5:18.
- How does our experiment remind you of this verse?
- What happens when you tell a lie? Do you ever have to tell another lie to cover up the first lie? Then someone else asks you about the same thing, and you lie again. It just keeps going!
- What happens when a kid bullies someone for the first time and no one says anything? When no one objects, then that first-time bully has permission to do it again…and again…and again. It just keeps going!
- God doesn't like lying. He doesn't like bullying. There are other things that just don't go along with being a Christian—things that God doesn't like. Usually, once you get started on one of those things, it just keeps going! What other ways can people go against God that seems to just keep going? (gossip, jealousy, arrogance)
- How could we have stopped the string of beads from continuing? (Someone would have had to step in and grab the beads.) How can we stop our disobedience of God? (We need to ask Jesus to step in and take hold of us! We need to admit that we're in this cycle and need Jesus to rescue us. He is the only One who can grab hold of our sin and help us stop.)

Other verses to use with this experiment:
- Romans 7:15
- 1 John 3:6-10

Hidden Potential
The future

Scripture:

Jeremiah 29:11 (ESV)
For I know the plans I have for you, declares the Lord, plans for welfare and not for evil, to give you a future and a hope.

Lab Equipment

- condiment cup with lid
- gel cubes (any color)
  (Gel cubes can be purchased from teacher supply stores and science websites. The jar I purchased about 10 years ago has thousands in it and cost under $10.)
- water

Experiment

- Place one gel cube in a condiment cup.
- Fill the cup with water and secure the lid.
- Leave it undisturbed for 18-24 hours.
- Remove the cap and look into the cup to see what's there.
- Gently poke your finger around in the cup and then lift the discovered cube from the water.

Observation

- Could you see the cube in the water?
- What had to be added for the cube to change?
- What is the difference between what went into the cup and what you pulled out?

- What was your reaction when you discovered what was in the cup?
- Use 5 words to describe what the cube was like when it came out of the cup.

Discussion for teachers and parents

- Read Jeremiah 29:11.
- How does the gel cube make you think of this verse?
- The tiny gel cube we placed in the cup yesterday represents a child. They are small when they are placed in our care.
- The cube we pulled out of the cup is what God has planned for that child. Could you see what was in the cup? (No, it was invisible when you looked into the water! God takes that little one and changes him or her into someone interesting and beautiful and surprising. You had no idea what was going to come out of the water.)
- The responsibility of parents and teachers is to add the water. We are to supply an environment that is conducive to children growing closer to God. We need to provide them with the spiritual nutrition that God will use to fulfill His plan in the children's lives. Our job is to "just add water."
- God gives us these children. He trusts us to point them to Him so they will live a life that brings Him glory. And, He reveals Himself to each one to lead each one to the fulfilling adventure He has planned.
- What can we do to supply the water for others to grow to be who God intends them to be?

Other verses to use with this experiment:
- Deuteronomy 6:6-9
- Psalm 139:13-16
- Proverbs 22:6
- 2 Timothy 3:14-15
- 3 John 1:4

Kool-Aid Bursts™ Launch
Evangelism

Scripture:

John 17:18 (ESV)
As you sent me into the world, so I have sent them into the world.

Lab Equipment

- Kool-Aid Bursts™ bottle
- play dough™
- regular-size drinking straw
- sharp scissors
- small drinking straws

Experiment

- Enjoy a yummy Kool-Aid Bursts™!

- Rinse the bottle and shake out all the water.

- Using a pair of sharp-tipped scissors, cut the hole a little larger until a regular-size straw will fit snuggly through it.

- Make a 1" rope from play dough and wrap it around where the straw enters the bottle. Press it against the straw and bottle to make a seal. This will keep air from passing through (clay works even better).

- Punch one end of the smaller straw into the can of play dough so that just a little play dough stays in the straw. This will act as a plug. (The smaller straw should slide easily into the larger first straw. The closer the smaller straw is to the size of the larger straw, without getting stuck, the better the outcome.)

- Drop the smaller straw into the regular-size straw with the plugged end up.

- With both hands, squeeze the center of the bottle quickly and the smaller straw will launch.

- Launch several smaller straws.

Observation

- How far did the straws go?

- Did the straws go in the same direction?

- Did all the straws go the same distance?

- Would you be able to launch pennies with the Kool-Aid Bursts™ Launcher? Would you be able to launch an earring?

Discussion

- Read John 17:18.

- How does our experiment remind you of this verse?

- Who is God sending to share His message? He is sending YOU and ME into the world to do the same thing. What is the message He wants us to share? God wants us to show the world how much He loves them. He wants the world to know that He loved each of us so much...even before we were born...that He already had a plan to save us from our disobedience. And, God wants us to show the world how His desire is for all of us to live and honor Him. We are sent!

- Where are we sent? (The kids will tell of places where they can share Jesus and people they can talk to about Jesus. Each time a child mentions a place or a person, expand on it a bit and then that child will launch his or her Kool-Aid Bursts™ rocket.)

- Launch a straw. You are SENT into your school!

- Launch. You are SENT onto your playground.

- Launch. You are SENT to your ball team.

- Launch. You are SENT to your cousins, your aunts, your grandparents, and all your family.

- Launch. You are SENT into your home.

- You are SENT all these places so you can show God's love and live a life that honors Him.

Other verses to use with this experiment:
- Isaiah 6:8
- Matthew 28:19
- Mark 16:15

Lava Lamp
Alive in Christ

Scripture:

Romans 6:11 (ESV)

So you also must consider yourselves dead to sin and alive to God in Christ Jesus.

Lab Equipment

- 1-liter clear plastic bottle
- Alka-Seltzer™
- food coloring
- funnel
- vegetable oil
- water

Experiment

- Use a funnel to fill the bottle about one-third full with water.

- Then, fill the bottle to <u>just BELOW the neck</u> with vegetable oil. Pour it in gently and keep the bottle still, so it doesn't take as long for the oil and water to separate.

- Let the bottle set until the oil and water have separated completely.

- Squeeze 10 drops of food coloring (any color except yellow) into the bottle. Wait for the food coloring to go through the layer of oil and mix with the water. (The experiment could stop right here, because this is fun to watch.)

- Snap an Alka-Seltzer™ into pieces and drop them one at a time into the bottle. You've just turned on your lava lamp.

Do not put the cap on.

- For extra fun, hold a flashlight lens against the bottom of the bottle, turn out the lights and turn on the flashlight.

Observation

- What happened when we put the oil and water together in the bottle?

- When there was only oil and water in the bottle, and it was completely settled, would you describe it as still or active, dead or alive?

- Describe what you saw when the food coloring was added. What did it change?

- What happened when the Alka-Seltzer™ was added?

- When the Alka-Seltzer™ released its little bubbles, what did it take with it? (Some of the colored water.)

- Describe the bottle after the Alka-Seltzer™ was added: still or active? Dead or alive?

Discussion

- Read Romans 6:11.

- How does this scripture remind you of this experiment?

- At what stage of the experiment would you describe it as "dead"?

- At what stage of the experiment would you describe it as "alive"?

- Through Jesus, when we confess our sins and ask Him to be our Savior, we become dead to sin. Sin no longer has power over us when we claim the power of the Holy Spirit. BUT, it's more than just not sinning…it's being alive in Christ! When you think of something that is alive, what do you picture in your mind? Something lying around napping? Or something jumping, dancing, wiggling, running, and smiling? I think of movement when I think of something being alive!

- When you are alive in Christ, how do you move? What do you do that's different than when you weren't alive in Christ?

- I could watch this lava lamp all day because it's fascinating and it never looks the same. When you follow Jesus—when you are alive in Him—He leads you on a fascinating adventure, and your days will never look the same.

- What can you do to show others you are alive in Christ? How can you use your movements to show others that you have a new life in Christ?

Other verses to use with this experiment:
- Romans 8:10
- Ephesians 2:5

Lift Up a Plate
Humble yourself

Scripture:

James 4:10 (NIV)
Humble yourselves before the Lord, and he will lift you up.

Lab Equipment

- 2 pieces of scrap paper (3" x 4")
- clear jar
- flat lightweight plate
- match
- paper towel
- water

Experiment

- Fold a full sheet of paper towel in quarters and get it wet. Squeeze out all the excess water.

- Lay the dampened paper towel in the center of a flat lightweight plate. (I like to use a plastic picnic plate.)

- Place a scrap piece of paper in the jar and turn the jar upside down. Press the mouth of the jar into the damp paper towel.

- Grab hold of the jar and lift. Nothing unexpected happens. The jar comes away from the plate.

- Now, try it again with one thing changed. Loosely wad up the other piece of scrap paper (no larger than 3" x 4"). Light a match and catch the scrap paper on fire. When it has a flame, drop it down into a jar. (A pickle jar, jelly jar, or canning jar work well.)

- Turn the jar upside down and press the mouth of the jar into the damp paper towel.

- The flame will go out. Wait for 3 seconds.

- Then, grasp the jar and lift it straight up. The plate should come with it.

Observation

- Describe what happened the first time you lifted the jar from the plate.

- Describe the paper when it was put in the jar the second time.

- What happened to the paper once the jar was turned upside down on the plate the second time?

- What were you able to do once the paper was burned up?

Discussion

- Read James 4:10.

- According to this verse, what has to happen before God can lift us up?

- What does "humble" mean?

- When we humble ourselves, we acknowledge—we admit—that God is so much greater than we are. We realize that we are nothing without God. He is great beyond our imaginations, and we are His people. When we humble ourselves before God, we admit that He is the One who is important, and what He wants is most important. Our desires are nothing compared to Him.

- If the jar represents God, the plate represents us, and the paper is our pride (how great we think we are). Discuss the difference between what happened the first time we raised the jar and the second time. We had to smother our pride (the paper) before God (the jar) could lift us (the plate) up. (You may want to put labels on the jar and plate so the representations can be reinforced with the words.)

- What kinds of things do we need to be lifted up from?

- Why do you think we need to humble ourselves before God can lift us up? The plate sure couldn't lift itself up on its own, and we sure can't rescue ourselves from our sin punishment all by ourselves. When we humble ourselves, we recognize who God is—our Creator, who is all-powerful. If we don't recognize God as all-powerful and the One who can lift us up, then why should He show Himself in that way? If you don't believe that God can lift you up, why would He?

Other verses to use with this experiment:
- 2 Chronicles 7:14
- Matthew 16:24

Lifting Up Praise
Preparing to worship

Scripture:

Lamentations 3:41 (ESV)

Let us lift up our hearts and hands to God in heaven.

Lab Equipment

- 20 oz. water bottle (empty and dry)
- chopstick
- uncooked rice

Experiment

- Fill the water bottle with rice.

- Stick the chopstick down into the bottle as far as you can. Give it a good stab.

- Now, try to pick up the bottle of rice with the chopstick. Hold on to the exposed end of the chopstick and pull up. Disappointment. The stick comes out.

- Remove the chopstick completely and put the cap on the water bottle. Tap the bottle against a hard surface, causing the rice to settle. Add some more rice and tap some more. Continue doing this until when you tap the bottle, the rice no longer settles. (Have a bottle prepared that has been setting for an hour or more. That helps it settle completely.)

- Thrust the chopstick into the bottle of rice again. If you're not strong enough or don't have a good enough grip, then hit the end of the stick with a rubber mallet.

- Hold on to the exposed end of the chopstick and pull up. This time, the chopstick should hold tight in the rice and make it possible for you to pick up the bottle of rice.

Observation

- What happened the first time we tried to pick up the bottle?

- What happened the second time we tried to pick up the bottle?

- What was difference between the two attempts to pick up the bottle?

- How would you describe the rice in the bottle on the first attempt?

- Describe the rice on the second attempt.

Discussion

- Read Lamentations 3:41.

- How does this experiment remind you of the verse we just read?

- How can we lift up our praises?

- Does our praise go very far when we're not really serious about it? Name some things people do when a worship leader is leading the congregation in praising God. (They can be passing notes, checking their phones, writing something down, looking out the window, thinking about what they're going to do that afternoon, trying to stop kids from pestering each other, etc.)

- What do you think is on the mind of someone whose praises are really being lifted up? (Nothing is on his or her mind except how awesome God is and how much He deserves being praised.) Just like tapping the bottle of rice to get rid of the extra air and make it settle, we prepare ourselves by getting rid of the extra thoughts that are in our minds.

- How can you prepare yourself to praise and worship?

- When people are serious about praising God, it feels different than when they just go through the motions. Praises are being lifted up! When we worship God...all out...you can sense His presence.

- I want to be a believer who lifts praises to God and is crazy in love with Him!

Other verses to use with this experiment:
- Psalm 24:4-7
- Isaiah 40:26

Light and Relight
Resurrection

Scripture:

Luke 24:6-7 (ESV)
"He is not here, but has risen. Remember how he told you, while he was still in Galilee, that the Son of Man must be delivered into the hands of sinful men and be crucified and on the third day rise."

Lab Equipment

- 2 identical tall clear cylinders
- baking soda
- half-cup measure
- hydrogen peroxide
- lighter
- teaspoon
- tongue depressor
- white vinegar
- yeast

Step 1

Experiment

- Place half a packet of yeast in each of two tall, clear cylinders.

- Place a tablespoon of baking soda in each of the cylinders.

- Swirl the cylinders so the powders are mixed well.

- Pour ½ cup of vinegar into one of the cylinders. It will bubble up. You need your container to be tall enough that the bubbles do not reach the top of the cylinder.

- Pour ½ cup of hydrogen peroxide into the other cylinder. Again, this will bubble up.

- Light one end of a tongue depressor and let it burn for 10-15 seconds to prepare for the experiment. The tongue depressor needs to have a strong flame.

- Lower the lit tongue depressor into the cylinder with the vinegar. Do not touch the bubbles, but get the stick as close as possible. The flame will extinguish.

- Move the tongue depressor to the cylinder with the hydrogen peroxide. Lower the extinguished end down into the cylinder and get close to the bubbles without touching them. You'll see the stick begin to glow and then the flame will relight.

- You should be able to go back and forth–lighting and relighting the stick several times.

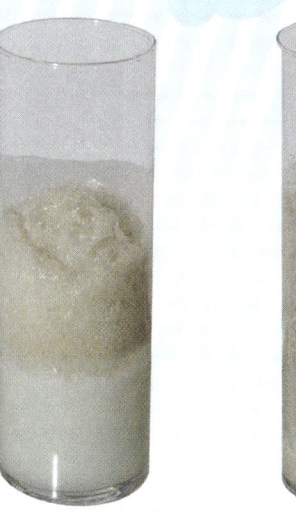

Step 2

Observation

- What happened to the tongue depressor when it went into the first cylinder?
- Did it stay extinguished? Did the flame stay out?
- How did the tongue depressor relight? Did it do so on its own?
- How did you feel when the stick relit?

Discussion

- Read Luke 24:6-7.
- Now that you've seen the experiment, how does it remind you of this well-known scripture?
- Which cylinder reminds you of Jesus' death?
- Which cylinder reminds you of Jesus' resurrection?
- Was it a surprise to you that the stick relit?

- When Jesus died on the cross and was buried, Satan thought he had finally won over Jesus. But, God's power surprised Satan. Jesus did not stay dead. On the third day Jesus came back to life.

- The Light of the World–a name that Jesus called Himself–had not been extinguished! Not even death could keep the Light of the World down.

- How did you feel as you waited to see what would happen to the extinguished stick when it was put in the second cylinder? You were on the edge of your seats, weren't you? The disciples and other followers of Jesus didn't know what was going to happen next in their lives or their ministries. They were trying to figure it out, waiting for a sign that would tell them what was next.

Other verses to use with this experiment:
- John 11:25-26
- Acts 4:33
- 1 Corinthians 15:3-5

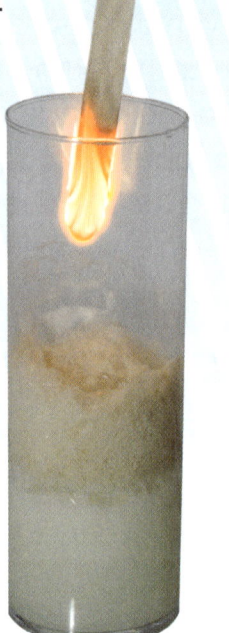

Step 3

Light Bulb in Microwave
Living in the Light

Scripture:

1 John 2:10 (ESV)

Whoever loves his brother abides in the light, and in him there is no cause for stumbling.

Lab Equipment

- clear glass (wide)
- light bulb
- microwave
- water

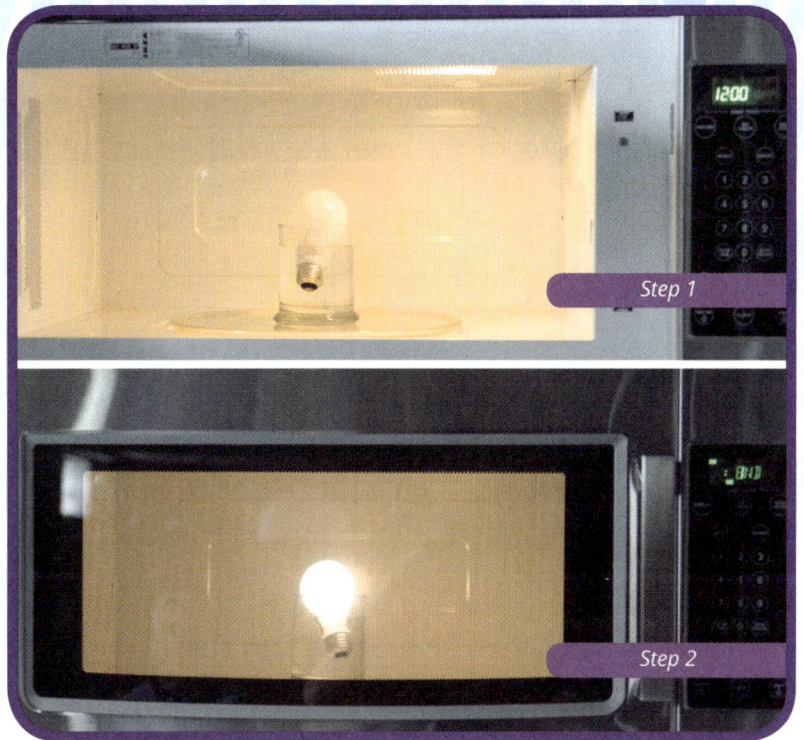

Experiment

- Fill the glass halfway with water.

- Remove the plate and anything else that is in the microwave.

- Place the light bulb, metal threaded cap down, in the glass of water and set it inside the microwave.

- Close the door and turn the microwave on HIGH.

- It usually takes about 5 seconds for the light bulb to light up. Turn the microwave off after the bulb has been lit for 3 seconds.

Observation

- What was the inside of the microwave like when we started?

- What happened in less than 5 seconds?

- How long did the light bulb stay lit?

- It wasn't plugged into anything, so where did the power for the light come from?
- Will it work more than once?

Discussion

- When we turn out the lights and try to walk around, what usually happens? It's easy to run into something, get our toe caught on the edge of a piece of furniture, or trip over a shoe that was left in the hallway.
- Who is called the Light of the World?
- Read 1 John 2:10.
- What does it mean to "abide in the light"? What does it mean to be "living in the light"? (It means we're so close to God we are able to show others what God is like. People who are living in the light honor God and the sacrifice that Jesus made. Their actions and words show others what God is like. If you're not living in the light, but claiming to, then you will stumble, and cause others to stumble–just like when the lights go out.)
- How can we keep from stumbling–giving into temptation?
- How can you bring light to a dark world? When you take time for someone who needs to talk, you are being light. When you are a friend to someone who has no other friends, you are being light. When you feed someone who is hungry, you are being light. (Each time one of these examples is shared, turn the microwave on and wait for the light bulb to light up before saying, "You are living in the light!")

Other verses to use with this experiment:
- Genesis 1:4
- John 9:5
- Ephesians 5:13

Forget Their Sins
God forgets our sins

Scripture:

Hebrews 8:12 (ESV)

For I will be merciful toward their iniquities, and I will remember their sins no more.

Lab Equipment

- hot water
- Memory Wire*
- pencil
- tall clear wide-mouthed container
- wire cutters

* Memory wire can be purchased from Educational Innovations (teachersource.com). This is not the same as the memory wire used to make jewelry.

Experiment

- Fill a tall, clear, wide-mouthed container (at least 12" tall) with very, very hot water. You will need it to be hotter than from the faucet–almost boiling.

- Cut a 10" piece of memory wire.

- Wind the wire tightly around a pencil, leaving 2" at the end to hold on to. Slide it off the pencil.

- Pull the wire out to straighten it with your hands. It's not necessary to get it straight, but just demonstrate that when you pull on both ends, the wire does not straighten completely.

- Wind the wire around the pencil again just like before, only this time it will be easier because it's already been wound and you couldn't get it straightened out completely. Remove the pencil.

- Watch closely, because this happens super fast! Holding on to the straight 2" at the end, poke the wound wire into the hot water. It will immediately straighten and go back to its original form. If you didn't get it all the way down into the water, then turn it upside down and submerge the part that didn't get straightened.

- You can demonstrate this repeatedly with the same wire.

Observation

- What form had the wire taken when we wound it? What was its shape modeled after?

- Were you able to straighten the wire completely with your hands?

- What happened when the wire touched the hot water?

Discussion

- Read Hebrews 8:12.

- How do you connect the verse and this experiment?

- When we wound the wire around the pencil, it took on the shape of the pencil. When we disobey God—sin—what shape do we take on? It's not the shape of God!

- When we accept Jesus as our Savior, confessing our sins and being forgiven by God, what does God do with our sin? He gets rid of it. He straightens us out! And, He forgets it when our last day comes and He judges us. He chooses

to mark off completely all the things we have done against Him. He marks off the times we have shown Him only disrespect. He marks off when we have chosen to follow Satan's instructions instead of His. The wire being placed in the hot water is a great picture of this.

- Does God have to think a long time about whether He's going to forgive you? No, it happens instantly, as soon as you ask. The wire took on the straight form immediately when it hit the water. We didn't have to watch for a long time and wait for it to happen. When it came in contact with the hot water, it straightened out. When we come in contact with God Almighty, the Creator of the Universe–confessing our sin and claiming Jesus as our Savior–He changes us immediately.

Other verses to use with this experiment:
- Isaiah 43:25
- 2 Corinthians 5:17

One Breath Confession

Scripture:

1 John 1:9 (KJV)
If we confess our sins, he is faithful and just to forgive us our sins, and to cleanse us from all unrighteousness.

Lab Equipment

- 2 Bernoulli bags (windbags) – 8' long. These can be purchased from **arborsci.com**, 4/$7, or at other science teacher supply sites.

Experiment

- You will need two Bernoulli windbags. Tie a knot in one end of each windbag.

- The leader who understands the experiment will take one windbag and give the other windbag to one of the kids. Shake out each windbag a little, since they have probably been pressed together during storage.

- Ask the kids observing to estimate how many breaths it will take to blow up one of the bags.

- At the signal, both the leader and the child will blow into the bag. The child will probably put the bag up to their lips, like you would a balloon, and start to blow. Let them huff and puff a couple of times before the leader blows into his or her bag.

- The leader should blow into the bag a different way. Hold the bag open using both hands. Your mouth should be about 6" from the opening. Take a deep breath and blow into the bag. You won't be touching the bag as you blow.

- After you have exhaled the one large breath, immediately close this open end to keep the air from escaping and slide the other hand down the windbag to compress the air into the tube. The bag will be filled.

- If you like, you can tie a knot in this end also to make a tube balloon that can be used for games or just to toss around.

Observation

- How many breaths did you think it would take to fill the bag?
- How many breaths did it take the kid who was blowing up their windbag?
- How many breaths did it take the leader to blow up the windbag?
- Describe the difference between the way the two people were blowing up their bags.
- Which was simpler to do?

Discussion

- Read 1 John 1:9.
- How do you think this verse relates to our experiment? (The kids will probably come up with several different ideas, so give positive feedback for their creative thinking.)
- When we blew into the windbag, we were exhaling air that was not good for our bodies. We were getting rid of it. How does that relate to 1 John 1:9? What are we getting rid of?
- How do we get rid of our sin? We have to confess it first. We can't try to do 3 good things to get rid of one sin. We just can't do enough good things to cover up the bad things. We have to confess. Having sin in our spirits is not spiritually healthy for us.
- What does confess mean to you?
- Too often, we talk about having a new life in Christ and how God is going to be with us when we make a decision to follow Him. And that is so true!

But, we can't go to that step without first going through the first step: to confess—to admit—that we have disobeyed God. When you confess, you have to look at your life and realize when and where you have acted in a way that would not please God, or when you have said things that are against His Word. You have to breathe out. You have to exhale the sin!

- Sometimes, people think it's a lot more involved than it really is. They think they have to work and work at it to get God to forgive them of their sins. That reminds me of our volunteer who huffed and puffed and tried to fill the windbag.

- But, in God's Word, He simply says to confess and He will forgive. Say the verse again, and point out how it's pretty plain and simple. It doesn't say that you have to do this…and wait this amount of time…and then go talk to this person and tell them what you've done…and then write down everything that was said…and then….No, no, no! Just confess, and He will forgive.

- Then, once we confess, God will fill us with all the good things that go along with His character.

Other verses to use with this experiment:
- Luke 13:3
- Acts 3:19

Ping-Pong® Wiggle
Unity

Scripture:

1 Corinthians 1:10 (ESV)

I appeal to you, brothers, by the name of our Lord Jesus Christ, that all of you agree, and that there be no divisions among you, but that you be united in the same mind and the same judgment.

Lab Equipment

- 2 drinking straws
- 2 ping pong® balls
- blow dryer
- clay

Experiment

- Place two mounds of clay, side-by-side, 1"-2" apart, on a flat surface near an electrical outlet.
- Stick a drinking straw into the center of each mound. Wiggle it side to side a little bit, to make sure the straw will be able to move slightly during the experiment.
- Stick a thick clay cap on each of the ping pong® balls.
- Push each of these onto the end of one of the straws.
- Hold a blow dryer pointing down in between the ping pong® balls.
- Turn on the dryer.
- Turn off the dryer.

Observation

- What happened when the dryer was turned on? (The balls came together.)

- What happened when the dryer was turned off? (The balls went back to their original position.)

- Is this what you expected to happen? When you blow on something, it usually goes away from you, not toward you.

Discussion

- Read 1 Corinthians 1:10.

- What does it mean to be united? What is unity?

- How does this experiment remind you of this verse?

- The scripture encourages believers to be united–to come together and not live in disagreement. We are not supposed to let things come between us as Christians and as the Church.

- What is it that brings Christians together? What is the main thing that we can all agree on? (Jesus Christ, God's Son, came to be our Savior and to bring us back to God.)

- When the blow dryer was on, the ping pong® balls came together. Let's think of the air coming from the blow dryer as the Holy Spirit. When we rely on the Holy Spirit to be part of all our relationships between our brothers and sisters in Christ, He will help us figure things out. He will help us come together so we can live in unity. Sometimes, just getting along feels like the most difficult thing in the world. Relying on the Holy Spirit and constantly turning our lives over to the way God wants to lead us can bring us together even when it seems too difficult to do.

- When the blow dryer was turned off, the ping-pong® balls moved away from each other. How is that like the way we rely on the power of the Holy Spirit? When we don't include the Holy Spirit in our relationships, it's hard for people in the Church to have unity. The power to do that isn't there if the Holy Spirit isn't invited into each situation.

- How do you feel when you're living in unity with other people? How do you feel when you know there isn't unity with the people around you?

- What do you think people outside the Church think when they see the Church doing everything in unity? What do you think people outside the

Church think when they see the Church arguing and not getting along?

- What one thing can you do that would help unity happen in your church?

Other verses to use with this experiment:
- Psalm 133:1
- Ephesians 4:3
- Philippians 2:2

Pull Harder
Nothing can separate us

Scripture:

Romans 8:38-39 (ESV)
For I am sure that neither death nor life, nor angels nor rulers, nor things present nor things to come, nor powers, nor height nor depth, nor anything else in all creation, will be able to separate us from the love of God in Christ Jesus our Lord.

Lab Equipment

- 2 phone books

Experiment

- Lay 2 phone books on a table with the raw pages up against one another and the spines facing away from each other. This really is easier to set up with 2 people working on it. You can actually use any 2 books—paperback or hard bound—as long as they are basically the same size.

- What you want to do is weave the books together. Slide the back covers over one another so that they overlap about halfway. Now, alternate a page from one book and then a page from the other book. Put down a page from the first book, and then a page from the second book. Keep doing it...keep doing it...keep doing it. You can do a couple of pages at a time, but not too many. Continue until all the pages of both books are woven together.

- Choose 2 people to demonstrate the experiment. The 2 will face one another and each will get a good grip on the binding of one of the books.

- Give a signal and let them have a tug-of-war with the books. Come on, pull them apart!

Observation

- What happened when the 2 people pulled on the books?
- Describe how the pages are put together.

- Maybe we needed 2 people who were stronger. Bring in 2 adults to demonstrate.
- How strong do you think you have to be to pull the books apart?

Discussion

- Read Romans 8:38-39.
- How does this experiment remind you of this scripture?
- What does the verse say can separate us from the love of God? Is there anything that could keep God from loving us?
- Do you think that if two trucks tied the books to their bumpers and pulled opposite directions that they could pull the books apart? Actually, this was tried on a TV show called *Mythbusters*, and the trucks could not get the books to come apart. It's because of a powerful force called friction.
- What power keeps us from being separated from God? His love is so strong—off-the-charts strong—that we can't even imagine how great His love is. When we believe with every breath we take that Jesus is our Savior and Lord, God says, "I will never leave you." People may try to pull you away from God…situations may pull on you and make you question God, but God's love is stronger than any of that.

Other verses to use with this experiment:
- Psalm 18:2
- Isaiah 40:29-31

Make a Joyful Noise
Praise

Scripture:

Psalm 98:4-6 (ESV)
Make a joyful noise to the Lord, all the earth; break forth into joyous song and sing praises! Sing praises to the Lord with the lyre, with the lyre and the sound of melody! With trumpets and the sound of the horn make a joyful noise before the King, the Lord!

Lab Equipment

- ½" PVC
- ½" PVC elbow joints
- ½" PVC T-joint
- plastic grocery bag
- rubber band
- scissors

Experiment

- PVC is very inexpensive, so get a bunch! You'll need to cut the 8-foot pieces into a variety of lengths (4"-10" long). There is a special tool for cutting PVC that is both inexpensive and very easy to use. Don't bother to measure the lengths…just chop away. Each kazoo will need about 6 pieces.

- Cut a piece of plastic grocery bag in about (and I say ABOUT—please don't measure this) a 4" diameter. If you're going to be making a bunch of kazoos, then layer about 10 bags on top of one another and cut them out at the same time.

- Place the plastic over the top of the T-joint and pull it down around the sides. Secure it by wrapping a rubber band around it until it keeps the plastic taut across the T-joint opening. This is the membrane that causes the kazoo vibration.

- Randomly put PVC pipe and elbows together to make an interesting configuration.

- Attach the T-joint at one end. This is the mouthpiece. (You can also add a little piece of PVC pipe to the front end of the mouthpiece, so you're not

getting the excess plastic on the membrane up your nose!)

- Hum into the mouthpiece and you're making wonderful music!
- Encourage the kids to name the instrument they have made— wrap-around-a-zoo, tooter-zoo, praiset, kazone.
- If you'd like, you can add ribbons to the PVC to give it a personal touch.

Observation

- Does your kazoo look like your neighbor's kazoo? How are they alike? How are they different?
- What was difficult about making the kazoo?
- Does the kazoo have to be a specific size to make a joyful noise?
- Does the kazoo have to look just like everyone else's to make a joyful noise?
- How do you get sound to come out of the kazoo?
- Hum a familiar song together. Describe what it sounded like.

Discussion

- We can call this an instrument, but it really isn't until one last thing is added. What is that? You!

- Have the kids rewrite Psalm 98:4-6 to include the name of their instrument.

- What changes music into praise? Your attitude, the condition of your heart, what you want to express to the Lord…are all things that change the sounds an instrument makes from just notes, honks, and hums into sweet sounding praise that makes the Lord smile.

- What if you decided to never blow into your kazoo? Could we still call it a praise instrument? It's not the instrument that God enjoys; it's YOU playing it to express your praise that He enjoys!

Clean-Up Tip:

When you're done with the PVC kazoos, take the mouthpieces off and set them aside. All other pieces can be disassembled and put in a supply tub. The mouthpiece, though, should be taken apart. Discard the plastic membrane. These are so easy (and free) to make that you don't need to try to clean them. Keep your rubber bands. Then, put the T-joint pieces in the dishwasher, and they'll be ready to reuse.

Other verses to use with this experiment:
- Psalm 33:3
- Psalm 81:1-2
- Psalm 150:4

Rising Match
Heaven

Scripture:

1 Thessalonians 4:16-17 (ESV)

For the Lord himself will descend from heaven with a cry of command, with the voice of an archangel, and with the sound of the trumpet of God. And the dead in Christ will rise first. Then we who are alive, who are left, will be caught up together with them in the clouds to meet the Lord in the air, and so we will always be with the Lord.

Lab Equipment

- match box
- wooden matches

Step 1

Experiment

- Empty the box of matches.

- You'll be using the inside cardboard box. Set the sleeve aside. Turn the box that was on the inside upside down.

- Poke a small hole toward one end of the box, just big enough to insert one match. You want the match to stand up. Push the match through the hole, so it is perpendicular to the box. If your hole is a little bit too big and the match won't stand up straight, add a ball of play dough underneath to hold the match in place.

- Lean another match against the one that is inserted in the box, so that they are at about a 30° angle from one another. The ends that you ignite should be touching one another, with the leaning one slightly on top of the one mounted in the box.

- Now, light a new match and place the flame against the center of the matchstick that is leaning. You want to catch the center of the stick on fire—not further down toward the end, near the box.

- Once the center of the leaning matchstick is on fire, the flame will move toward the touching ends, igniting both matches. Watch as the end of the leaning match that is against the box rises.

Step 2

Observation

- What did you expect to happen to the matches?
- Describe what happened to the leaning match.
- Did the matches separate or did they stay together?
- Which match seemed to join the other one?
- What was holding the match up in the air?

Discussion

- Read 1 Thessalonians 4:16-17.
- How does this experiment illustrate these two verses?
- The Bible tells us that some day Jesus will return. He will come down from heaven, so think of the match that came down into the box as Jesus. But, why will Jesus return? There is a purpose, and these verses tell us. He will return to gather up everyone who believed in Him. And we will meet Him in the clouds. Both the dead and the living will rise. Just as the match that was leaning on the main match, those people who have been leaning on Jesus—who have believed in Him—will rise, will meet Him in the air, and will always be with the Lord.
- Where will we rise to?
- How does it make you feel to know that if you live for Jesus, He will some day come to get you and make you rise to heaven—to a place that is so magnificent you can't even imagine its greatness? That will happen after you have

lived your life completely. He will take you to be with Him in a place far more wonderful than anything you could have in this life!

- Open your Bible again and read the next verse—verse 18. How does that verse say we should feel about this? (It should encourage us!) Why would it encourage us? (No matter what is happening now or how bad a situation gets, following Jesus will always lead to a day when He will come to take us with Him to heaven—to make us rise with Him.)

- What do you think heaven is like? It's hard to know what WILL be there, but we do know what WON'T be there. There will be no sickness...no bullies...no crying...no hurt feelings...no _____. You fill in the blank.

Other verses to use with this experiment:
- Philippians 3:20-21
- Revelation 21:3-4

Step 3

Separating the Egg
Separate from Sin

Scripture:

2 Corinthians 6:17 (NLT)
Therefore, come out from among unbelievers, and separate yourselves from them, says the Lord. Don't touch their filthy things, and I will welcome you.

Lab Equipment

- cheap empty water bottle
- raw egg
- small flat plate

Experiment

- Crack the raw egg and open it onto a small flat plate. Make sure you do not damage the yolk.

- Remove the cap from a water bottle. The cheaper water bottles work better because the plastic is thinner and can be squeezed more easily.

- Squeeze the bottle in the middle so the air is pushed out of it.

- While squeezing the bottle, place the mouth of it gently against the yolk of the egg.

- Slowly release the squeeze on the bottle. As you release the squeeze, the yolk will move up into the bottle and separate from the rest of the egg.

- If you want, you can increase the squeeze and the yolk will go back out of the bottle. You can go back and forth several times before the yolk weakens and breaks.

Observation

- Why do we have to be careful with eggs?
- How do people usually separate eggs?

- What happened when we stopped squeezing the bottle?
- What happened when we squeezed it again?
- Do you think this is a good way to separate eggs?

Discussion

- Read 2 Corinthians 6:17. How does this verse relate to the egg experiment we just did?

- According to this verse, what are we supposed to separate ourselves from?

- Why do we need to separate ourselves from sin?

- When we sucked the yolk up into the bottle, it was no longer part of the whole egg as it had been when it was on the plate. A person who is not a believer is part of a world of sin. When we confess and give our lives to God because of what Jesus did for us, then we're different…we're separate…we're not like everyone else. It doesn't mean we're not going to live next door to people who don't believe, but it does mean we will no longer be part of the sinful things we used to do. We separate ourselves from them and don't participate in sin anymore.

- Have you confessed to God how you have disobeyed Him? Do you act the same way as you did before you believed? Do you talk the same way?

- How have you been like the yolk of the egg and separated yourself from things that God would not be happy with? What have you said "No" to, because you knew it would mean disobeying God?

Other verses to use with this experiment:
- Proverbs 16:17
- 1 Thessalonians 5:22

Shrinky Dinky Cup
Under pressure

Scripture:

Daniel 3:17-18 (NASB)
If it be so, our God whom we serve is able to deliver us from the furnace of blazing fire; and He will deliver us out of your hand, O king. But even if He does not, let it be known to you, O king, that we are not going to serve your gods or worship the golden image that you have set up.

Lab Equipment

- pressure cooker
- small glass casserole dish
- Styrofoam™ cup
- stove burner
- water

Experiment

- Put about ½" water in the bottom of a pressure cooker and insert the raised metal plate that comes with the cooker.

- Set a small glass casserole dish on the metal plate.

- Place a Styrofoam™ cup in the center of the glass casserole.

- Lock the lid in place on the pressure cooker and don't forget to add the topper.

- Place on a hot burner for about 10 minutes. The pressure cooker will be steaming.

- Remove from the stove and let it set until the pressure has gone down. You can speed this up somewhat by spraying the pressure cooker with cold water. It is not safe to remove the lid until the cooker has cooled.

- Remove the lid and pull out the Styrofoam cup.

Observation

- What did the cup look like when it went into the pressure cooker?
- What did the cup look like when it came out of the pressure cooker?
- Will it hold the same amount of water after it's been through the cooker?
- Did the cup explode? Did it collapse?
- Which do you like better? The original cup? Or the shrinky dinky cup that's been through the pressure cooker?

Discussion

- Read Daniel 3:17-18. (You may want to read more [starting with verse 8], because these two verses are only part of the story of King Nebuchadnezzar throwing Shadrach, Meshach, and Abednego in the fiery furnace.)
- When the king threatened to throw the three men in the furnace, what did they say?
- Did they know they would survive—that God would save them?
- How much pressure do you think they were under, on a scale of 1 to 10, with 10 being a huge amount of pressure?
- How do you relate this story (especially verses 17 and 18) to our experiment?
- The three men went through a life-threatening experience—a lot of pressure—but they came out of it. How do you think the experience changed them inside spiritually? I can't imagine them not being changed in almost unbelievable ways! (And our cup was surely changed in an unbelievable way!) Who else could say they went into a burning furnace, with their hands and feet tied, and came out perfectly fine because God decided to do a crazy-big miracle? I bet that story came up in just about every conversation they had the rest of their lives!
- The men were committed to the Great God Almighty, and no amount of pressure was going to change that. You probably haven't been threatened with being thrown in a fiery furnace, but what causes you to feel pressured?

Do you feel pressure to go along with others when you question what they are doing? Do you feel pressure from your parents? Teacher? Coach?

- What do you think is a good way of handling that pressure? What one thing can you start doing when you feel pressure in a situation?

- It doesn't feel good at the time, but going through pressure and standing our ground with God changes us. It makes us into better Christ-followers. When you go through a difficult time knowing that God is with you, you come out better than the person you were before.

- You can be like the three men going into the furnace and say, "Even if things don't come out the way I want them to, I will not cave under this pressure. I will not stop relying on God! My God is greater than any pressure you can put on me!"

Another verse to use with this experiment:
- Zechariah 4:10

Spilled Out
Love spills out

Scripture:

John 13:34-35 (ESV)

A new commandment I give to you, that you love one another: just as I have loved you, you also are to love one another. By this all people will know that you are my disciples, if you have love for one another.

Lab Equipment

- 1 liter empty bottle with cap
- tarp
- thumbtack
- water

Experiment

- You will need to do this experiment outside, or if you do it indoors, you'll need a tarp or large tub.

- Fill the 1-liter bottle with water and screw the cap on tight.

- In various places around the bottle, less than 2" from the bottom, poke holes in the bottle using a thumbtack.

- Loosen the cap.

- Tighten the cap.

- Loosen the cap.

- Tighten the cap.

Observation

- What happened when you loosened the cap?

- What happened when the cap was on tight?

- How big do you think you could make the holes? What if you used an ice pick instead of a thumbtack to poke the holes?

- Taste what came out of the holes. (You should never taste anything in an experiment unless the person leading the experiment gives you permission.)

- If we didn't put any water in the bottle, what would happen when we loosened the cap?

Discussion

- Read John 13:34-35.

- Is there anything in our experiment that reminds you of this scripture?

- In the verse, something is supposed to spill out. What should spill out? Our love for one another!

- If we didn't loosen the cap, the water wouldn't come out. It could've been pop in the bottle, and we wouldn't have known it. It's not until it spilled out that we knew it was water. If we never demonstrate our love for other people, we can say that we have love inside of us, but no one knows if that's true, because it hasn't spilled out for us to taste it—experience it.

- Name some times when we "keep the cap on" and don't share the love of Jesus with others. Why do you back off from loving someone?

- Name some times when you've "loosened the cap" and let God's love spill out onto others. Do you think they knew that you loved them?

- If there's no water in the bottle, then none will spill out. What does that tell us about our relationship with God? We need to allow Him to refill us with His love. We do that through praying, reading the Bible to know what God desires, by talking with other Christians, watching how God is working in their lives, and by sharing in worship.

Other verses to use with this experiment:
- Proverbs 16:22
- John 7:38

Spinning Chair
Hold God close

Scripture:

James 4:8 (NIV)
Come near to God and he will come near to you.

Lab Equipment

- 2 16-ounce cans of vegetables, fruit, or whatever
- swivel chair (steno chair, not padded)

Experiment

- You'll need a swivel chair that spins very easily. Ones that are padded do not spin as freely. (In other words, the more uncomfortable the chair, the more likely that is what you're looking for.) You may want to squirt it with a touch of WD-40 to make sure it turns easily.

- One person will sit in the chair. He or she should extend both arms, holding one of the two 16-ounce cans in each hand. If the spinner can hold larger cans, that helps make the experiment more dramatic.

- Another person will give the chair a mighty spin.

- Once the chair begins spinning, the person in the chair should bring his or her arms to the chest, holding the cans up close. When this happens, the chair should spin faster.

- Putting the arms back out will slow the chair.

- Move them in and out and see what happens.

Observation

- How did we make the chair spin around?

- What happened when the spinner brought the cans to his or her chest?

- How did the spinner's arms feel when he or she brought the arms to his or her chest?

- Which way was more exciting—spinning with arms out? Or spinning with arms to the chest?

Discussion

- Read James 4:8.

- Share how this verse reminds you of the experiment you just did.

- Let's say that the cans represent God. When the spinner held the cans close to the chest, he or she was able to spin faster, which made us all squeal! God has an adventurous life for each of us—a life that will make us squeal with delight. But, in order to experience that adventure to the fullest, we need to hold God close. How do we do that?

- When do you feel God's presence the most? When do you hold Him closest?

- Tell about a time when you lived each day with God at a distance. We all have times when we think we can take care of everything on our own. We believe in God, but we're not holding Him close.

- Now, tell about a time when you held God close. How did your life change? What did you think about more often? What did you do more often?

- James 4:8 is a promise that God gives you and me. If you will hold Him close, He will hold you close, and give you the ride of your life!

Other verses to use with this experiment:
- Deuteronomy 10:20
- Hebrews 10:23

Stacking Surprise
Trust God

Scripture:

Proverbs 3:5 (ESV)
Trust in the Lord with all your heart, and do not lean on your own understanding.

Lab Equipment

- half sheet of copy paper
- hardbound book (storybook)
- miscellaneous objects
- tape

Experiment

- Hold a half-sheet of copy paper perpendicular to the table. Set a hardbound book on top of it and let go. The book will crush the paper.

- Very evenly, roll the half-sheet of paper into a tube (about the diameter of a toilet paper roll or a little bigger). Tape it securely, making sure the edges are even.

- Stand the tube of paper on the table. Set the same hardbound book on top of the tube, centering it. The tube will support the book this time. It's the very same piece of paper, though.

- Now, you can stack other things on top of the book, placing them in the center, right above the tube. (Imagine a line going up through this tower.)

For example: Put a juice glass on top of the book, then add another book, then a can of nuts, etc.

Observation

- What happened to the paper the first time we set the book on top of it?
- How did we change the paper?
- What happened the second time we placed the book on top of the paper?
- What made the paper stronger?
- How many things did you think we would be able to stack on the paper tube?
- How many things were we able to stack on the paper tube?

Discussion

- Read Proverbs 3:5.
- What should we NOT lean on? What should we lean on? Another way of saying "lean on" is to use the word "trust."
- What should we NOT trust? We can't depend only on what we know ourselves. None of us even begins to understand everything about our lives, the people around us, or the world we live in. If we think we can always "figure it out on our own," then we're leaning on ourselves or trusting in ourselves.
- Have you ever said, "Oh, I can do this myself"? Or, "I'll figure it out"? Who are you leaning on when you say those things? Who are you trusting when you say that?
- What does this verse say about how much you're supposed to trust God? It says "with all your heart," so that means with everything you've got. Don't hold back! Trust God with every decision, every relationship, every situation you're in. Yes, everything!
- Which part of the experiment do you think represents leaning on ourselves?

- Which part of the experiment do you think represents trusting in God?

- Which way was the paper stronger and able to hold more weight?

- When we trust in God completely, and wrap ourselves up in Him (like we wrapped the paper), we are going to be stronger and able to go through difficult situations in surprising ways. When we trust God, He will support us!

- What one thing can you trust God with this week? Give Him the thing that you've been thinking you could handle on your own without His help. See what happens when you trust Him.

Other verses to use with this experiment:
- Jeremiah 29:11
- Matthew 7:24-27
- Romans 8:28

Standing Broom
Stand up for your faith

Scripture:

1 Corinthians 16:13-14 (NASB)

Be on the alert, stand firm in the faith, act like men, be strong. Let all that you do be done in love.

Lab Equipment

- kitchen broom with angled bristles

Experiment

- On a smooth floor, set the broom bristles flat against the floor. Do not push them down; just let them rest there.

- Hold the handle between your flattened hands. You don't want it to lean either way. It will feel like it can't stand that way, because the handle will be going at an angle from the floor (about 55-60° angle).

- Gently release the handle from your hands. If it tips over, you haven't gotten the handle straight. You'll feel it sustain itself when you pull your hands away when the bristles are flat against the floor and the handle is straight. It will stand on its own!

Aside:

One day when walking through a Target store, I saw new brooms on the end-cap. I couldn't resist! I pulled one out...got it to stand on its own in the middle of the aisle...and then walked off.

Observation

- Describe getting the broom to stand on its own.

- Did it stand the very first time? How many tries did it take before the broom stood on its own?
- What was needed in order for the broom to stand on its own?
- What is the reaction of other people when they see the broom standing by itself?

Discussion

- Sometimes, we have to take a stand for our faith in Jesus, and it feels like we're the only one. When have you stood up for what you believe?
- How did you feel when you were the only one taking a stand? What made you feel like you just couldn't go along with the others?
- What kinds of things are important to take a stand about?
- Read 1 Corinthians 16:13-14.
- How does this verse remind you of the broom?
- What do we need to do daily in order to be able to "stand firm in the faith" when the opportunity comes?
- When is it easy to stand firm in your faith?
- What does verse 14 say about your attitude when you feel you must take a stand?

Other verses to use with this experiment:
- 1 Corinthians 15:58
- 2 Timothy 2:15

Stomp Rocket Witnessing

Scripture:

Acts 1:8 (NLT)

But you will receive power when the Holy Spirit comes upon you. And you will be my witnesses, telling people about me everywhere–in Jerusalem, throughout Judea, in Samaria, and to the ends of the earth.

Lab Equipment

- 10-foot piece of ½" white PVC (not tan CPVC)
    - 36" piece of ½" PVC (lays on ground)
    - 21" piece of ½" PVC (launching piece that rocket fits over)
    - 12" piece of ½" PVC (joins 90-degree connector and cross-tee)
    - two 21" pieces of ½" PVC (legs)
- one 90-degree ½" rigid non-metallic conduit connector
- two 45-degree ½" rigid non-metallic conduit connectors
- ½" straight coupler (connects the 36" piece to the 90-degree connector)
- ½" PVC cross-tee (comes up from 90° connector and legs attach with 45° connectors)
- two ½" PVC end caps (for the ends of legs)
- cap from 2-liter bottle
- clear packing tape
- duct tape
- empty 2-liter bottle
- file folder
- globe
- plastic wrap
- PVC cutting tool

Making the Rockets

- Open and flatten a cardstock file folder. Cut a piece that is 15" long and 3½" wide. The length of the rockets will be 15".

- Roll the 15" length around a ½" piece of PVC pipe. You want it to be snug, but loose enough that it will slide off the PVC easily. Tape along the seam with

clear packing tape to hold the piece of folder in the tube shape.

- Slide the tube off the PVC.

- Make a ball of plastic wrap a little smaller than a ping pong® ball. This should fit in one end of the rocket. Leave some of it sticking out, because this will provide cushion when the rocket hits the ground on descent and will prevent the rocket from being crushed. Cover the plastic wrap ball with duct tape to finish this protective tip.

- Go ahead and make several now, so you don't have to chase one rocket after each stomp.

Assembling the Stomp Rocket

- Cut the pieces of PVC to size according to the lab equipment list. The photo below and descriptions next to each supply should tell you how to assemble it.

- At the very end of the PVC where the 2-liter bottle fits on, you will want to mount a cap from a 2-liter bottle. Drill a ½" hole in the top of the cap and push it barely onto the end of the PVC. Then, use duct tape to secure it. When a bottle is stomped-out and needs to be replaced, you can simply screw a new one in place, rather than reattaching the entire cap and bottle.

Experiment

- Secure a 2-liter bottle on the end of the rocket launcher. Leave the label on the bottle, because this will be a guide for where to stomp.

- Stand on one side of the rocket launcher. Raise one foot high and then come down across the label, as if your foot were going

around the bottle. You do NOT want to stomp on the bottom of the bottle or it will need to be replaced each time. If you stomp across the label, your bottle should last 40-50 stomps.

- See how high you can make the rocket go. Stomp away!

Observation

- What had to happen in order for the rocket to launch?
- What affected how high the rocket went?
- Did the rocket go off one direction, or did it go straight up and back down?
- How many times do you think we could launch the rocket?

Discussion

- Read Acts 1:8.
- Which of the places listed in this verse did the stomp rocket remind you of– Jerusalem, Judea, Samaria, or the ends of the earth?
- What does it mean to be a witness? (Being a witness means to share with someone else what God has done in your life.) How is your life different than it was before you accepted Jesus as your Savior?
- According to this verse, who are we supposed to witness to? Jerusalem is where they were, so we are supposed to be witnesses in our own town. Judea and Samaria were like going into our counties and states, a little further than our city. It means that when we have the chance, we can witness to people who aren't right in our backyard. But what does "the ends of the earth" mean? It means that we have a responsibility to tell others...even on the other side of the world...about Jesus. These are people we don't know and may never get a chance to meet. We still need to find ways to witness to them.

- What are people in other countries like? Why might it be difficult to witness to them? What would we have to learn about people at "the ends of the earth" before we could witness to them? People in other countries speak a different language, so knowing their language well would be important. Some other things you need to learn in order to witness is how the people feel about family, if work is important to them, if their good manners are the same as ours, if they are offended by the same things we are, and if they worship a false god. Can you name more things you'd have to learn in order to effectively witness?

- Look at a globe and name a place that feels like the "ends of the earth." Then, give a stomp on the stomp rocket as the kids all yell, "To the ends of the earth!"

Other verses to use with this experiment:
- Matthew 28:19
- Acts 22:15

Suspended Support
Bear one another's burdens

Scripture:

Galatians 6:2 (ESV)

Bear one another's burdens, and so fulfill the law of Christ.

Lab Equipment

- 3 butter knives
- 3 identical bottles
- plastic juice glass (even though the picture shows a can)
- water

Experiment

- Fill a plastic juice glass with water. Hold a butter knife by the handle and place the glass on the blade of the knife. See if you can balance it there.

- You will need 3 identical bottles. If you use plastic bottles, you will want to add some water to weight them down a little. Glass bottles have enough weight that you won't need to add anything. Position the bottles in a triangle with about 6" between them. The distance will vary depending on how big around the bottle is.

- Hold 3 butter knives in a triangle, overlapping the blades. Each blade should weave on top of one knife blade and underneath another knife blade. This locks the blades together in a triangular shape with the handles sticking out.

- Rest a handle of each of the connected knives on the top of a bottle. This is where you may need to adjust the distance between the bottles. You want each handle to rest across the center of one of the bottle openings.

- Once you have the knives suspended from the bottle tops, set a glass in the center where the knives intersect.

- Fill the glass with water.
- For additional fun, see how big a glass of water the knives will support!

Observation

- Were you able to balance the glass of water on the blade of one knife? If you could, how comfortable were you with doing that? How difficult was it?
- What did you have to do to the knives to get them to suspend from the bottles?
- What happened when you set the glass of water on the three knives?
- What amazed you about this experiment?
- How long do you think the knives will hold the glass in the air?

Discussion

- Read Galatians 6:2.
- How do you connect this scripture to the fun experiment we just did?
- When you tried to balance the glass of water on one knife, you may have been able to do it for a few seconds, but it sure wasn't comfortable. What if that were the only way you could hold that glass?
- Let's imagine that when you did this it represented you trying to carry your burden all by yourself. Now, what is a burden? It's something difficult that you're going through. Maybe you have an illness or someone you're very close to is ill. Your burden may be that you have difficulty learning at school, or maybe someone is bullying you. Your burden may be that you're trying to live in two different households because your mom and dad are no longer together. What are some other burdens kids have? Going through any of those things is really difficult when you feel like you're all by yourself.
- Galatians 6:2 says we're supposed to help carry each other's burdens. When all three knives were woven together, they supported one another, AND they were miraculously able to support the heavy glass of water. It sure wasn't as difficult as trying to balance the glass on one knife all by itself.

- What does it mean to "carry someone's burden"? It can mean being the person who listens to them when they're angry, frustrated, confused, or sad. It can mean you're the person who checks on them each day to see how they're doing. It can mean inviting the person to do something with you so they can get their mind off their problems. It can mean defending someone. It can mean telling someone who can be more helpful. What are some other ways kids can carry each other's burdens?

- Sometimes we think we know what would help someone, when really there is something different we could do that would be a lot more comforting and helpful. When you say, "Is there anything I can do for you?" it's hard for someone to tell you what they really need. But, if you have an idea of what you could do, then say, "Here's what I'd like to do for you. Would that be okay, or is there something else that would help you more?" Then the person knows you're really thinking about them and want to help.

- What can you do this week to help carry someone's burden? How can you let someone know that you're there to help them?

Other verses to use with this experiment:
- Ecclesiastes 4:7-12
- Romans 15:1
- 1 Thessalonians 5:11

View from above

Swinging Bucket
Trust God's Word

Scripture:

Titus 1:9 (ESV)
He must hold firm to the trustworthy word as taught, so that he may be able to give instruction in sound doctrine and also to rebuke those who contradict it.

Lab Equipment

- bucket with a strong handle
- drop cloth
- mop (just in case)
- water

Experiment

- Lay down a drop cloth in the area where you will conduct this experiment. Make sure the space has a high ceiling.

- You will need someone who has fairly strong arms and endurance, so the experiment can continue for a little while. Have this person practice with an empty bucket at first, making sure he knows what to do, and is able to do it. He should hold the bucket at his side, using his dominant hand. The motion he needs to master is swinging the bucket in a circle, from down by his side, straight up, and then back down (pivoting his shoulder so the bucket goes behind him). Do this several times, so he feels the bucket pulling away from him as he swings it. (Think: Ferris wheel.)

- Now, fill the medium-sized bucket a little over halfway with water.

- Hang it to the swinger's side, just like he did with the empty bucket. Then, begin the swinging motion. Don't start out slow. He needs to get it going immediately.

Keep the bucket moving in a circle.

Observation

- How did the swinger get the bucket started?
- What do you think would've happened if the swinger had slowed down his swinging motion?
- How much water did the swinger lose?
- What surprised you about this experiment?
- Describe how the swinger held the handle while he was swinging.

Discussion

- Read Titus 1:9.
- What in this verse reminds you of the experiment we did with the swinging bucket?
- What do we need to hold firm to? (God's Word! We must trust what we learn from the Bible.)
- According to this verse, what do we need to be able to do? (We need to be able to teach others about God's Word and to help people understand some things they believe are not from God.)
- How do we prepare ourselves to help others understand God's Word? How will we know if they believe something that isn't true? The only way is to get to know the Bible by reading it, listening to what good godly teachers have to say, asking questions, asking God to show us what He means, and memorizing it so that it's in our minds at all times. In other words, we've got to spend time getting to know the Word!
- You can trust God's Word to be the truth, so hold on to it tightly...just like our swinger held on tightly to the swinging bucket!

Other verses to use with this experiment:
- Romans 12:9
- Philippians 2:16
- 1 Thessalonians 5:21
- Hebrews 10:23

Temptation Sand
Temptation

Scripture:

Galatians 5:1 (ESV)
For freedom Christ has set us free; stand firm therefore, and do not submit again to a yoke of slavery.

Lab Equipment

- 2 clear plastic punch cups
- ½ c. water
- Magic Sand (find this at 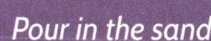stevespanglerscience.com)
- teaspoon
- thin craft stick

Experiment

- Start with a cup that is about 2/3 full of water.

- In a separate cup, put about 3 tablespoons of the Magic Sand.

- In a steady stream, pour the Magic Sand into the cup of water, right in the center. It will make an interesting sand sculpture in the water.

- Now, slowly pour the water out of the cup until you think you have poured it all out of the sand.

- Gently jostle the cup of sand back and forth and you will see more beads of water appear at the top. Pour those off. Jostle the cup again and you'll probably have more appear. Keep doing this until there are no more beads of water appearing.

- Let the children touch the sand. It will be dry just like it was before you poured it in.

Pour in the sand

Observation

- What did you expect the sand to do when it was poured into the water?
- Describe what the sand looked like in the water.
- After the water was poured off the sand, what happened when the cup of sand was shaken a little more?
- What happened when the cup of sand was shaken a second time? A third time?
- What did the sand feel like after the water was poured off? Was it wet, or damp, or dry?

Discussion

- Read Galatians 5:1.
  Satan is going to tempt us—going to try to get us to disobey God—but what does this verse tell us to do?

- Redo the experiment, but this time, talk the kids through it. Let's say the sand represents each time Satan tempts us. What are kids tempted to do? (cheat on a test, take something off a store shelf, copy music without permission, lie about what happened). Each time the kids name one of their temptations, add a teaspoon of the Magic Sand to an empty cup.

Pour out the water

- Satan makes temptations look attractive, interesting, and sometimes even beautiful to us. Pour the sand into the water. This made an attractive, interesting, beautiful design. Surely, there's nothing wrong with that...and that's just what Satan wants you to think.

Shake

When your parents are proud of you because of the better grade on your report card, cheating on the test doesn't seem so bad. When you don't get grounded because you covered up with a lie, the lie doesn't feel so bad.

- Temptation is Satan's way of talking us into sin. You've got to get away from it. If a friend is constantly trying to talk you into doing things you know aren't right, then you need to get away from that friend. Remembering scripture will help when you're tempted. What other things will help you when you're tempted? Pour the water off the sand.

- Sometimes, you think you can leave just a little temptation and sin, if you get away from most of it. But, you need to get rid of ALL of it. Get away! Shoo! Flee! Shake the sand and pour off some more water. Keep doing that until it's all gone. Don't mess around, holding on to even a little temptation in your life.

- God wants you to be pure and clean, free from sin and away from temptation. He wants you to STAND FIRM when it comes to following Him and not give in to whatever Satan is trying to get you to believe.

- Read Galatians 5:1 again. Encourage the kids to write the verse in their own words, now that they've practiced the experiment.

Other verses to use with this experiment:
- Matthew 6:13
- Luke 22:40

Unbreakable
Relying on God's strength

Scripture:

Psalm 28:7 (ESV)

The Lord is my strength and my shield; in him my heart trusts, and I am helped; my heart exults, and with my song I give thanks to him.

Lab Equipment

- 2" x 4" board – 18" long
- 4 stemmed goblets
- one-step stool

Experiment

- Set a stemmed goblet on the floor and ask if anyone thinks he or she can stand on it without causing it to break.

- Set 4 identical goblets side by side in a row on the floor. Then, place a 1" x 4" x 18" long board across the top of them (or relatively similar in size).

- Set a one-step stool behind the goblets. Choose someone to step up on the stool and then take a step onto the board. If the child is small enough, you can pick her up and set her on top of the board so there's no stepping on to it. This is just to make sure the glasses don't move under the board.

Observation

- What do you think would've happened if someone tried to stand on one goblet?

- What offered strength and stability to the goblets so someone could stand on them?

- What do you think would happen if we only used 3 goblets with the board? Try it. What do you think would happen if we only used 2 goblets with the board? Try it.

Discussion

- Read Psalm 28:7.

- How does this scripture remind you of the experiment we just did?

- If we would try to stand on one goblet by itself, that would be like trying to live on our own strength. What happens when we depend on ourselves for everything and don't depend on God? We could easily get crushed!

- In our experiment, the board was added across the top of the glasses to make it possible to stand on them. It added strength to the goblets. So what would you say the board represents?

- God gives us promises in His Word. When we believe in and depend on those promises, we can say that we're "standing" on them. What are some of the promises of God?

- When have you said, "Oh, I think I can handle this on my own. I don't need Your help, Lord"? You decide you can live on your own strength rather than relying on God's strength. That's like removing the board! What happens then? There's a mess!

- When you consult God on your decisions—EVERY decision—then you are relying on His strength. What decision have you consulted God about?

- To be spiritually strong, we need to know what we believe and then rely on God's strength to get us through and help us stand.

Other verses to use with this experiment:
- 1 Chronicles 16:11
- Isaiah 41:10
- 1 Peter 4:11

Upside Down
Jesus brings change

Scripture:

Acts 17:6 (ESV)

And when they could not find them, they dragged Jason and some of the brothers before the city authorities, shouting, "These men who have turned the world upside down have come here also."

Lab Equipment

- 4" x 4" piece of cardboard
- juice glass
- water

Experiment

- Fill a juice glass about ¾ full with water.

- Cut a piece of cardboard about 4" x 4". You want to make sure it is not wrinkled or corrugated on the surface.

- Pick up the juice glass in one hand and lay the cardboard square across the top of the juice glass with the other.

- Gently press the cardboard against the glass with the tips of your fingers in a circle over what is approximately the rounded edge of the glass.

- Now, flip the glass upside down, holding the cardboard against the glass with your fingertips.

- Hold the glass completely vertical and then pull your fingers away from the cardboard. The cardboard will stay in place and the water will not come out.

Step 1

Observation

- What did you think when the person flipped the glass upside down?

- What was the reaction of the person holding the glass when he or she was told to pull his or her fingertips away from the cardboard?

- What happened to the cardboard when the person let go of it?

- What did you think was going to happen when the fingertips were pulled away?

- What do you think would have happened if the glass was tilted and it wasn't completely vertical—straight up and down?

Step 2

Discussion

- Read Acts 17:1-8.
  Paul and Silas are in Thessalonica, preaching about Jesus—His life, death, and resurrection.

- What does verse 4 say happened to some of the people when they heard?

- What does verse 5 say happened when the Jews heard?

- How does verse 6 describe what was happening when people heard about Jesus? (The world was turned upside down!)

- What does it mean that the world was turned upside down? Did everyone go around looking at everything upside down?

- Put your head down in between your knees and look around the room. Everything looks completely different, doesn't it?

- When people admit their disobedience to God and accept Jesus as their Savior, their lives change. They look at things differently.

They have a different attitude. They treat others differently. Things that were important are no longer so important. It's like their lives have been turned upside down!

- The message Paul and Silas had was turning the world upside down. It was changing everything! Our message today is the same, and we can turn our world upside down when we tell others about Jesus.

Other verses to use with this experiment:
- John 3:17
- John 8:32

Water Stream
Unity

Scripture:

Psalm 133:1 (ESV)
Behold, how good and pleasant it is when brothers dwell in unity!

Lab Equipment

- 2-liter bottle
- cap
- index card
- push pin
- water

Experiment

- Fill a 2-liter bottle with water and cap it tightly.

- About 2" up from the bottom of the bottle, insert the push pin (thumb tack) through the bottle.

- Move to the right of this hole about 1/8" and insert the push pin again. Do it a third time, moving to the right another 1/8". You should have a row of 3 tiny holes in the 2-liter bottle, but they will not be leaking water.

- Loosen the cap and the water will start flowing from all 3 holes.

- Get your thumb and index finger up close to the bottle and "pinch" the 3 streams of water together. When you let go, they should make one stream instead of three. (You can also do this by grabbing the water streams in your fist.)

- Is there anything you can do to separate the streams of water again? Try putting an index card or a small piece of plastic between the individual streams up close to the bottle. Pull it away to see what happens.

Observation

- What caused the water to start flowing?
- How many streams of water did we have to begin with?
- How did they become one stream?
- Do you think you could've just thought about them becoming one stream and they would have?
- What happened when you put something between the individual streams of water? Were they able to stay together or did they separate?

Discussion

- Read Psalm 133:1. (This is a good verse to memorize.)
- What does "unity" mean? (Unity is when separate things are brought together for a common purpose.)
- For what purpose were these 3 streams brought together?
- How does this scripture remind you of our experiment?
- Why is unity a good thing? What makes it a pleasant thing?
- As brothers and sisters in Christ—as believers in Christ—what should bring us together? Why should we have unity?
- As Christians, what is our common purpose?
- What things cause us not to have unity? What can we do when there is no unity? What do other people (people who don't believe in Jesus) think of Christians when we are not unified?
- What things bring us together, just like the streams of water were brought together?
- When we keep our thoughts, our attitudes, our goals, and our actions—as individual people and as a church—all focused on Jesus; then we can live in unity. When we get selfish and want our own way, or we see other things as more important than the message of Jesus, then we have trouble living in unity.

Other verses to use with this experiment:
- Ecclesiastes 4:12
- Matthew 18:20
- Philippians 1:27

Scripture Index

1, 2, 3

1 Chronicles 16:11	145
1 Corinthians 1:10	105
1 Corinthians 7:17	65
1 Corinthians 10:13	28
1 Corinthians 11:1	60
1 Corinthians 15:3	55
1 Corinthians 15:3-5	96
1 Corinthians 15:58	130
1 Corinthians 16:13-14	129
1 John 1:9	31, 102
1 John 2:10	97
1 John 3:1	59
1 John 3:2	37
1 John 3:6-10	79
1 John 4:7-8	48, 59
1 John 5:3-4	29
1 John 5:18	78
1 Peter 3:15	19
1 Peter 4:8	32, 48
1 Peter 4:11	145
1 Peter 5:1-5	62
1 Thessalonians 4:16-17	113
1 Thessalonians 5:11	137
1 Thessalonians 5:21	140
1 Thessalonians 5:22	117
1 Timothy 6:10	26
2 Chronicles 7:14	90
2 Corinthians 1:20	49
2 Corinthians 4:7-9	22
2 Corinthians 5:17	36, 101
2 Corinthians 6:17	116
2 Corinthians 9:8	18
2 Corinthians 12:9-11	13
2 Peter 1:4	50
2 Timothy 2:15	130

2 Timothy 3:14-15 81
2 Timothy 4:18 41
3 John 1:4 81

A

Acts 1:8 .... 75, 131
Acts 3:19 104
Acts 4:33 96
Acts 10:34 59
Acts 14:22 15
Acts 17:6 146
Acts 17:27 45
Acts 19:28 66
Acts 22:15 134

C

Colossians 3:12-15 48
Colossians 3:22 30

D

Daniel 3:17-18 118
Daniel 3:19 68
Deuteronomy 4:1 30
Deuteronomy 6:6-9 81
Deuteronomy 10:20 125

E

Ecclesiastes 3:1-8 8
Ecclesiastes 4:7-12 137
Ecclesiastes 4:12 151
Ecclesiastes 7:9 68
Ephesians 2:5 87
Ephesians 3:20 16
Ephesians 4:3 107
Ephesians 4:11 63

Ephesians 4:31 68
Ephesians 4:31-32 32
Ephesians 5:13 98
Ephesians 5:15 10

G

Galatians 3:26-28 58
Galatians 5:1 141
Galatians 5:24 43
Galatians 6:2 .... 35, 135
Genesis 1:2 74
Genesis 1:4 98

H

Hebrews 8:12 99
Hebrews 10:23 .... 51, 54, 125, 140
Hebrews 13:5 26
Hebrews 13:7 62

I

Isaiah 1:18 32
Isaiah 6:1 72
Isaiah 6:8 84
Isaiah 31:5 74
Isaiah 40:26 93
Isaiah 40:29-31 109
Isaiah 41:10 .... 42, 145
Isaiah 43:25 101
Isaiah 55:9 71
Isaiah 57:15 72

J

James 1:2 15
James 1:2-4 21
James 4:8 .... 45, 124
James 4:10 88

Jeremiah 29:11 .... 80, 128
Job 30:13 26
John 3:17 148
John 6:44 40
John 7:38 123
John 8:32 148
John 9:5 98
John 10:10 18
John 11:25-26 96
John 12:32-33 38
John 13:15 48
John 13:34-35 121
John 13:35 46
John 13:37-38 11
John 16:33 15
John 17:18 .... 77, 82
Joshua 1:9 .... 14, 24

L

Lamentations 3:41 91
Luke 2:52 10
Luke 13:3 104
Luke 22:40 143
Luke 24:6-7 94
Luke 24:47 57

M

Mark 16:15 84
Matthew 2:9 73
Matthew 6:13 .... 28, 143
Matthew 6:19-21 26
Matthew 7:24-27 128
Matthew 11:28-29 27
Matthew 16:24 90
Matthew 18:20 151
Matthew 19:21-22 25
Matthew 25:14-30 70

Matthew 25:35-40 33
Matthew 28:6 69
Matthew 28:19 . . . . 84, 134

P

Philemon 1:6 57
Philippians 1:27 151
Philippians 2:2 107
Philippians 2:4 35
Philippians 2:16 140
Philippians 3:20-21 115
Philippians 3:21 37
Philippians 4:6-7 28
Philippians 4:13 24
Proverbs 3:5 126
Proverbs 13:20 62
Proverbs 16:17 117
Proverbs 16:22 123
Proverbs 19:11 68
Proverbs 22:6 81
Psalm 18:2 109
Psalm 18:32 24
Psalm 24:4-7 93
Psalm 28:7 . . . . 24, 144
Psalm 33:3 112
Psalm 71:2 42
Psalm 81:1-2 112
Psalm 98:4-6 110
Psalm 103:10-12 32
Psalm 119:133 . . . . 51, 54
Psalm 119:171 52
Psalm 133:1 . . . . 107, 149
Psalm 139:13-16 81
Psalm 140:1 42
Psalm 145:4 57
Psalm 145:18 40
Psalm 150:4 112

R

Revelation 21:3-4 ... 115
Romans 2:6-8 ... 30
Romans 6:11 ... 85
Romans 7:15 ... 79
Romans 8:10 ... 87
Romans 8:17 ... 57
Romans 8:28 ... 128
Romans 8:38-39 ... 108
Romans 12:2 ... 37
Romans 12:3-8 ... 65
Romans 12:9 ... 140
Romans 15:1 ... 35, 137

T

Titus 1:9 ... 138

Z

Zechariah 4:10 ... 120

Notes

Notes

Notes